TOPBARBER

Live Your Dream.

Tracy Love

BE A TOPBARBER

All rights reserved. No part of this publication may be reproduced, distributed, or transmitted in any form or by any means, including photocopying, recording, or other electronic or mechanical methods, without the prior written permission of the publisher, except in the case of brief quotations embodied in critical reviews and certain other noncommercial uses permitted by copyright law.

Although the author and publisher have made every effort to ensure that the information in this book was correct at press time, the author and publisher do not assume and hereby disclaim any liability to any party for any loss, damage, or disruption caused by errors or omissions, whether such errors or omissions result from negligence, accident, or any other cause.

Adherence to all applicable laws and regulations, including international, federal, state, and local governing professional licensing, business practices, advertising, and all other aspects of doing business in the US, Canada, or any other jurisdiction is the sole responsibility of the reader and consumer.

Neither the author nor the publisher assumes any responsibility or liability whatsoever on behalf of the consumer or reader of this material. Any perceived slight of any individual or organization is purely unintentional.

The resources in this book are provided for informational purposes only and should not be used to replace the specialized training and professional judgment of a health care or mental health care professional.

Neither the author nor the publisher can be held responsible for the use of the information provided within this book. Please always consult a trained professional before making any decision regarding the treatment of yourself or others.

Copyright © 2024 by Tracy Love
ISBN: 978-1-7360276-4-6

Dedication

This book is dedicated to my family – Sherah, Kaaria, Tory, Jaedyn, Ryan and Riley for their ongoing love and support throughout my entire career. Everything I do, I do it for you. I love you guys forever.

Table of Contents

Introduction 1

Section One
Creativity & Inspiration

Chapter One - *Inspiration* 7

Chapter Two - *Creative Power*...............................15
    Create Your Flow
    Creative Push
    Healthy Habits
    You Are Who You Surround Yourself With

Section Two
The Barbershop and You

Chapter Three – *Being a Barber* 26
    The Up, The Down, Full Circle Moments
    For all my Female Barbers

Chapter Four – *The Barbershop* 37
The Hair Industry
The Barbershop and You

Customer Service

Chapter Five – *Finding the Right Barbershop* 43
Cut Everyone!

Finding a Shop (Questions)

    Shop Business
    Shop Scene
    Shop Environment
    Shop Expectations
    My Experiences

Chapter Six - *Being Self-Employed* 84
Building Your Credit
Medical Insurance
Accidental Insurance
General Liability
Retirement
Saving Tips
File and Pay Your Taxes

Section Three
Beyond the BarberShop

Chapter Seven - *Starting a New Creative Direction* 102
    Be a Mobile or Freelance Barber for Sports, Music, TV/Film or Agency
    Starting a Business
    Marketing
    Branding

Chapter Eight- *Hair Shows* 124

Chapter Nine - *The Entertainment Industry* 134
    Surrounding Yourself with the Right People
    How I Got Started in the Music Business
    From the Barbershop
        To the Industry
        Sean is my Kanye
    The Most Important Rules
     Loyalty
     Separate your personal life and work life
    Don't take anything personal!
    Work Ethics
    Making it work
     Maintaining Shop and Celebrity Clients
    Handling the Pressure

Chapter Ten - *The Business Side* 161
    Understanding Your Value
    Financial Management
   Setting Your Rates for
    Housecall Rates
    Travel Rates
    Set Rates
     Creating Invoices
   On The Go for
    Life on Set/Housecalls/Travel
    Industry Options
      Work for Yourself or Get an Agent
    The Union for Film and Television

Chapter Eleven ....…..185
    From the Heart

INTRODUCTION

Maybe you are a new barber to this amazing creative industry, maybe you have been in the profession for 10 years already, or maybe you are just thinking of entering the field. Whatever part of the journey you are on, my hope is this book will inspire you, give you some insight on different opportunities and answer a lot of the questions you may have had throughout your career.

I have been very successful in this incredible industry, and I would love to share my experiences with you—the good and the bad, the successes and the failures. I have worked in three barbershops, a full-service hair salon, a major beauty chain, and six years as a platform artist in the hair show business for Andis, one of the biggest clipper companies in the world. I have also worked for more than 10 years and continue to work in the entertainment industry as a barber and male groomer for some of the biggest music artists that have believed in my talents and have ultimately changed my life. I also work with reputable music labels such as Interscope, Sony Music Entertainment, RCA and Universal Records, where I continue to pick up newer artists as well.

And, along with writing this experienced based book that I hope to inspire you and the generations to come with, I have finally launched my newest adventure, my barber/male grooming agency called Topbarber Agency. Where we send barbers and groomers out to do housecalls for celebrity clients or work on production sets doing music videos, photoshoots, commercials, editorials, red carpets and more. This is my newest love because not only is it the first barber/male grooming company out there, but it is also opening up a whole new avenue of opportunities for other barbers who have the same talent and passion that I do.

My life is very unpredictable. I usually work long hours and the pressure can be overwhelming, but I wouldn't change it for the world. I am extremely proud of all my accomplishments in the entertainment industry, I worked very hard for it, but I also really love the barbershop; it is where I get all of my love for this profession, where my normalcy comes from, and where my passion lies. To me, the barbershop is where the culture lives. I work in a great barbershop close to home with some amazing barbers that I have grown to be real good friends with. They are my shop family, full of great laughs, good times, lessons, and love.

I also have a lot of great supportive clients, some of whom have been there with me from the beginning, that I really appreciate and that I am thankful for. A lot of good people come through there, and everyone is welcome.

Although I'm really busy, always tired, and things can get super hectic, I love everything about the barbershop and this incredible profession, and I know that I am blessed to have such an amazing career.

Along with that writing this book is a huge part of my life purpose, and I am excited to share it with someone who shares the same passion and strives toward the same goals. This book is intended for the barber who is looking to be at the top of their game, the barber who is looking to create a successful journey, the barber who is wants to set themselves apart from the rest and make a difference, the barber who ultimately wants to be a Topbarber. My goal is to give you the creative inspiration to follow your dreams, and my hope is this book will inspire you to take pride in your work, help you push your limits, and become successful in this industry you have so much passion for.

There are a lot of inspiring messages, lessons and valuable information inside this book and I encourage you to read it all, but it is designed to help you wherever you are in your career, so if you come to a chapter that doesn't apply to you feel free to skip it, but if and when you need it, it will always be there for you to come back to.

Even though my inspiration for writing this book is based on my love for barbering, I have over 20 years of experience in the amazing hair industry, and I hope that what I've learned along the way can help you. After all, in doing hair we all provide an amazing life-changing service with every client, and we all have bigger goals we want to attain that are intertwined with our strong desire for this awesome career.

So, if the direction you are heading now is new to you or you feel like you need a creative push, you will find inspiration, guidance, and growth in this book to help you be legendary in whatever path you decide to take.

This is a very powerful profession. It takes creativity, dedication, consistency, and most of all, passion. It ultimately changes who you are and even better, changes the people's lives you touch every day.

> Remember: No matter what, you have the ability to attain whatever it is you want in your life. All you have to do is want it badly enough, so stay focused and have no doubt and no fear, and God and the universe will put the people and opportunities in your life to make whatever it is you want to happen. Do not stop believing in yourself and what YOU are capable of!

SECTION ONE:

CREATIVITY
&
INSPIRATION

"The Highest Human Act Is to Inspire."

Chapter One
Inspiration

There are more ways than one to be a Topbarber. Yes, working for my agency is one way. But to be a Topbarber means more than that, it means you are creating your own pathway, following your own journey, pushing through all your obstacles, and creating success. Whatever that is for you. Your vision of success will not be the same as everyone else, and whatever your dreams and life goals are, will only be the most important to you. And there is nothing wrong with that. Being a Topbarber comes with the mindset of achieving whatever YOUR passion and purpose is, not everyone else's. Being happy and successful at what you love and are passionate about while contributing your life purpose to society is ultimately what it is all about. It is what makes the world go around, I believe it is why we are here. Being a barber is a special career but being a Topbarber means you understand your purpose and you will stop at nothing to achieve it.

Once you are a barber, choosing a creative path within this industry may be something you want to think about. Unknown to some you can take many different routes in the hair industry. Maybe you want to open your own barbershop, take your talents to the entertainment industry, join the union for film and television, be a platform artist and travel to different hair shows, work for a specific product company, or even create one! Or maybe you simply want to just work in a barbershop and be the forever-lasting, everyone-knows barber.

This is a career that is full of different avenues of inspiration and opportunity. It all depends on you and finding what you like doing just as much as cutting hair. It may take some time, but I guarantee once you are in a shop cutting hair for a while you will get a creative desire to take your career a step further, so line up your goals and get ready to turn them into something you can be proud of!

First, follow your curiosities...all of them and stick with the one you can't live without. This may take quite a bit of brainstorming, plus it can be a trial and error trying to figure it out, but this is to be expected. Remember, overcoming obstacles is normal, it teaches you resilience and every lesson is valuable.

Like me, you may think you have an interest in something, but you discover halfway through it that you like it, but you don't necessarily have a passion for it, so you lose interest and move on. Or maybe you created something, and it didn't get as much attention as you planned, so you lost the excitement and let it go. It's okay, don't be nervous or discouraged by this. It's normal to try a couple of things that interest you and you figure out shortly after it wasn't what you wanted. This may be the very way you find your next idea or creation that takes your career to the next level.

For me, I started to create a travel bag to make my life easier when I'm on the move traveling or doing house calls. I shortly discovered that I didn't mind making one for myself, but I wasn't sure if I wanted to create a business out of it. However now that I have a grooming company, more than likely, I will go back and create one for the Topbarber team. People always said I should open my own shop, but I knew the amount of work it takes to do that and make it successful, and right now I don't have the time. I am not saying never, but I know it is not for me at this moment. I also made an oil for hair and beards that I love using on my clients, but I have no passion to start a product line. Basically, none of these things excited me the way cutting hair did. I knew once I figured it out, it would be something that I would feel passionate about, and it would be something that I couldn't stop thinking about.

After all, there's a bigger goal we all need to accomplish for ourselves to fulfil our ultimate purpose that can teach and inspire other people along the way.

The things that I have accomplished in my career I really aspired to do, and I worked hard to achieve it. I have always been driven to accomplish my goals no matter the obstacles. I was undeterred by the people who didn't believe in me or tried to stop me; they actually made me more focused. I know that if I had let them stop me, I would not be the person I am or be where I am today. And most likely I wouldn't have even written this book. I have learned to always bet on yourself, and you will never lose. So, if you have a passion for something you want to do, or bigger goals you want to achieve, believe in yourself, and don't let anyone distract or stop you; you can do it!

Throughout my career, it has taken me a long time to figure out what I wanted to do next. I have achieved so much success and have accomplished many of my aspirations, but for some reason, I still felt unfulfilled. I knew there was still something that I wanted and needed to do. For me, I had to ask myself some questions and I had to seriously think about what it was that that was missing in my life. I knew that once it hit me, I would be instantly inspired, and I would know it immediately. It was like I could feel it right there, but I just couldn't put my finger on it. There were a lot of questions that I would often think about over and over again before I finally figured it out, which was:

* What could I do that I would love doing as much as cutting hair?
* What else could I do that would make myself proud?
* What could I do to set myself apart from everyone else?
* What could I do to inspire other people?
* What could I do that I haven't done yet?

Questions like these would just flow in and out of my mind all the time, and I could never answer them. But I believe it's okay to not have every solution there when you need it; this is what makes us strive for our answers and grow with our intention. Plus, I believe timing is everything, and it is always perfect.

One day, March 31, 2019, to be exact, it finally came to me! Not too many people know the inspiration for this book came from the death of Nipsey Hussle, a modern-day philanthropist. I was so inspired by his tenacity and his mindset. He was such a genuine and respected person to so many people and was always giving back without seeking recognition for it. When he died, people of all classes, cultures, and ages came out and spoke about how he changed their lives.

He had so many projects he was doing to encourage the youth and contributed to better his community. Everyone had their own story of what he did for them and why they loved him; he was so inspiring to me. He made me realize my purpose wasn't fulfilled yet, and in my heart,

I wanted to be the same way. I felt like there was something bigger than me that I needed to achieve to ultimately fulfil my purpose here on earth. And although he's gone way too soon, in some ways I feel his purpose in life was fulfilled as the inspiration he left will carry on forever through me and others he's touched that will ultimately serve a greater purpose. He said something that changed my life and motivated me to write this book:

"The highest human act is to inspire."

I saw this and I thought, He's right. How can I inspire people? What is it that I'm supposed to be doing here on earth to ultimately fulfil my purpose? How can I leave a legacy? How can I reach my full potential? And it came to me—write a book! But honestly, people have told me before that I should write a book, and I always thought, what would I write? And where do I even start? But this time, it was like a light switch turned on, and as soon as I thought about it, all these ideas and thoughts just started flowing into my head. I couldn't stop them, and I couldn't write them down fast enough. I was so excited; I grabbed my pen and my energy and heart immediately flowed right onto paper! I knew it instantly, and I couldn't believe that I finally figured it out. It took a lot of time and thought, but here it is! You are now reading it! People ask me all the time how I made it to where I am and what better way to share my thoughts, experiences, and advice than to write a book. However, I know that sounds great, but it wasn't easy. I didn't even know where to start other than to just start, and let me tell you, this was probably one of the hardest, yet most rewarding things I have ever done in my entire life.

I sincerely hope this book inspires you, enhances your creative purpose, and helps you reach your full potential.

The bottom line should be to decide it and become it.

> *Being a creative person is something to be proud of it is one of the best superpowers in the world, it is a gift and should be used to its fullest ability.*

Chapter Two

Creative Power

This is a creative industry, and as you start your career, you will be looking for ways to grow, expand, and tap into your creativity. For that reason, I wanted to touch on your creative power and give you some tips on how to tap into it when you need it the most and help you apply it to your career.

Creative people make the world go around. Creative people bring peace and sanity to the world, believe it or not. It's quite interesting if you think about it. We cut and style hair, but it's actually alot deeper than that; when people look good, they feel and perform at their best. We make the difference if they have the confidence to get the job they are striving for or that date they are seeking, which in turn could turn into a well deserved job or wife.

Being a creative person is something to be proud of; it is one of the superpowers in the world, it is a gift and should be used to its fullest ability. After all, creative people made amusement parks, community parks, museums full of art, and pretty much all the recreational things we like to do on the weekends or on our days off that relax us and allow us to enjoy our free time. Even down to the sporting events we watch to entertain us. All of these types of physical and mental getaways are mandatory for us to balance our lives. Thank God for creativity and all the people who have a passion for it.

Because of the pursuit of balance and change, it isn't a surprise that creative people can get bored or an itch to do something else that stimulates their minds. It's almost expected, so if you have been doing hair for a while now and you're looking to do something else with your talents, do it!

Your talents don't stop expanding just because you found what you are passionate about; instead, it sometimes opens the door for you to venture out and create something new for yourself. You are capable of doing anything you set your mind to, remember that! If you feel the need to create or feel something is missing in your life, maybe you should do something about it. It starts with an idea, maybe you want to create a product or tool, open a barbershop, start a podcast or create a brand of your own.

I say whatever it is, start thinking it, talking about it, empower your vision, feel your own creative power and begin to manifest the next milestone in your life!

Create your Flow
As a creative, you have many opportunities and directions you can take in this industry. Just let your passion drive you. This process can seem tedious, repetitious, and at times can seem challenging, but it

is also a learning and rewarding experience. Keep a positive mindset, believe in yourself, and trust me it will all be worth it. Remember to enjoy the process.

At the end of the day, it will broaden your experience and allow you to embrace your craft. Best of all, you can celebrate your wins even if they're small, appreciate how far you have come, and be grateful for where you end up even more.

If you are having a hard time thinking of what's next, don't worry. We can tend to overthink—that's all a part of being someone who creates. We can have creative blocks, which is perfectly normal, so don't get frustrated; it will come to you. Blocks are a hindrance to creatives because it feels like our minds stop and we can't express ourselves. These blocks can be helped by incorporating positive thoughts and healthy habits, but most importantly, be patient and remember that timing is everything.

If you feel stuck, keep your mind open because it's important for creative people to stay motivated and inspired to keep the creative juices flowing. The goal is to create a momentum that will move you towards success, so don't get discouraged; stepping out of your comfort zone, creating a brand, a new company, or even the beginning of a new idea is not easy.

Remember, you should be just as passionate about your new business venture as you are about barbering.

Take your time during this process.

Creative Push

If you are feeling uninspired and like you can't come up with something that grabs and keeps your attention, the good thing is you can do some simple things if you feel you are at a standstill with your thoughts or motivation to be more creative. These things will help you think outside your box and set yourself up for success.

The first thing you can do to stimulate your creativity is to expand your horizons. Try traveling, reading books, attending things of interest such as going to museums, movies, or art exhibits. Explore all things of interest that ignite your creative energies and get your mind flowing. We as creatives are influenced by sights, sounds, and feelings. We take what sparks our fire and we bring it to life. There is no limit to a creative mind, so don't be afraid to expand and enhance it.

Another thing is to learn from the experts in your current field or your field of interest. Don't we as creatives often look to the best in our industry—our mentors—to learn new techniques to incorporate into our work and to come up with new ideas?

Learning from other people can help motivate, educate, and give you an inspiring creative push in the right direction to help you transform and embody your vision. Remember, it doesn't matter if you are just starting or a seasoned pro, sometimes the best source of creative inspiration comes from others.

A really good creative rule is when a moment of inspiration presents itself to you—get on it! At that moment, plan around your most demanding idea, the idea that you can't stop thinking about; write it down and keep track of any and all ideas during moments like these because creativity is a muscle that can be developed with constant exercise and healthy habits. It's something that can take time before anything really creates a spark. But everyone and everything around you should inspire creativity; you just have to open up to it.

And don't forget to live in the moment; this will calm your mind, allowing you to find space to think clearly, tap into your natural intuition, and create a positive appreciative state that helps create an energy that spills into your ideas and life.

"Imagination is the beginning of creation.

You imagine what you desire, you will what you imagine,

and at last, you create what you will"

- George Bernard Shaw.

Healthy Habits
Being healthy and forming healthy habits can really spark your creativity, relieve stress, and increase your productivity. One of the most important things that should be at the top of your healthy habits list is to get up early in the morning and start creating!

The most successful people you know and are inspired by are up at five in the morning getting things done. This is a time when your brain is more alert, so you can get a head start before everyone wakes up. This will increase your productivity and allow you to work without interruptions. Along with waking up to get an early start, use these healthy habits to spark your own great ideas:

* Grab a coffee or your favorite beverage.
* Have a light, healthy breakfast to kick start your metabolism and fuel your body.
* Workout! Even just a light walk--getting some vitamin D from the sun boosts your mood and creative thinking.
* Meditate regularly to help yourself brainstorm, think, dream, and power down consistently to keep your powers of creativity strong.
* Unplug. Rest helps foster new creative connections.
* Keep a notebook to increase creativity as well. It helps to get into the habit of collecting and saving your creative ideas. It allows you to immediately write them down as they come to you, so you don't forget them, and it also frees up mental space and energy for other thoughts and tasks. So, write it down and track your brainstorms. You will not only retain your ideas longer, but you will have more of them as well.

These are just a few things that you can incorporate into your everyday life to help expand your creativity. Even if you just start with a few of these healthy habits, you will see a big difference, starting with your thought process. I have noticed that if you are a creative person, it never just stops after you have created something; you keep going because there's always more you want to do.

You Are Who You Surround Yourself With

I am surrounded by some of the most creative people and teams of people who make the magic happen. This inspires me to work hard and not give an excuse to say something can't be done. My experiences have taught me to remain focused and keep pushing forward no matter what. Because this is such a fast-paced industry and things are constantly changing, the last thing you want is to be caught standing still without a plan.

Getting to know many successful people through this business has allowed me to learn from some of their experiences as well. I hope to share as much as I can with you, so you can take it and apply it to your own life and career. When you learn through the experiences of others, it can save you a lot of time and heartache, and it gives you a much broader perspective. Yes, this industry can be tough, but it will make you a stronger person who works hard and appreciates even the smallest of things.

This is important to recognize because, through all of my successes and that of the people around me, we know that the more we are grateful for and appreciate everything we have, the more we will be blessed with things to be grateful for.

Living in the moment, as I mentioned earlier, is one of the most important things you can do without a doubt because along with a lot of other benefits, it helps relieve stress and overthinking. Also, thinking creatively through inspiration helps to keep your mindset positive and puts you into a creative state where you are the most productive.

Surrounding yourself or engaging with people you aspire to be like or who have the habits you are looking to acquire changes everything. It is known to improve your perspective in your life as well as your personal and career successes. It will ultimately inspire you to expand your mind, step your game up, and help you reach your goals much faster. These people give you energy and fuel your mindset into being great.

Surrounding yourself with positive successful people helps us to consciously and subconsciously challenge ourselves into being our best self. You will find that they live in the moment, and more often than not, they practice healthy habits, are openminded, optimistic, confident, encouraging, and are very mindful people.

I can speak from my own experience from being around some very successful great minds that always inspire me to practice gratitude, push myself, be open-minded, include healthy habits and keep positive thoughts in my daily routine, so I can stay motivated and continue to grow and move to my next level. It's always about forward progress.

I also find that reading books and expanding my knowledge is key to me having a better insight into my life, and it also expands my thoughts to help me think more creatively, ultimately helping me to become a better me. Hopefully, after you read this book, it makes you a better you.

Creativity takes time and energy but should be extraordinarily fun. The funny thing about creativity is that the more you do it, think it, write it, or use it, the more you have it. Taking advantage of other people in their creative works will not only keep your inspiration alive, but you will grow tremendously as an artist and person.

Remember, you can do anything you set your mind to, but even better, you can do anything you commit your heart to.

It doesn't matter what part of your journey you are in, I guarantee at some point in your career you will want to do more. You are a creative! So, if you think you are done once you have discovered your passion for doing hair, this is just the beginning!

Inspiration can take you a long way, so when you are ready to start expanding your talent and grow as an artist, be excited, get creative and keep going!

SECTION TWO:

The Barbershop and You

> No matter what, when the wins are happening it is important to take the time to live in those great moments; these are milestones, so they need to be recognized.

Chapter Three

Being a Barber

Before we get started in navigating your career, I wanted to touch on the power of being a barber. It is a superpower if you are strongminded and willing to work hard. Being a good barber takes consistency and it is something you have to work at every day. This industry can feel overwhelming at times, but it can also be the most rewarding because we do change lives, and honestly, whether you are male or female in this industry we are all going to undergo our ups and downs and at times we will experience self-doubt; however, speaking from my experience, as being a female barber, it has had its own difficulties, but nothing a little strength and persistence can't handle. All of my experiences throughout my career have taught me something, and they have created the person I am today. No regrets here.

There is a strong pride that comes with being a barber. We eat sleep and breathe haircuts and we take our profession very seriously. So being a barber is something I have always been proud of. Without a doubt I knew this was what I wanted to do from the moment I picked up a pair of clippers. And I also knew in the beginning it was going to be a challenge because this was a male-dominated industry, and I didn't know any female barbers at the time, but I knew I wanted to change this image and work hard to become one of the best. I wanted to be in demand and respected for my talent.

At the time I had no other goals in mind other than to set a fair standard between women and men in this industry, and in my mind I knew this would be a challenge because I often thought that some men may not want a woman to cut their hair or I also thought how could I compete with a guy that is personally familiar with what a man would like when it comes to personal grooming, but I never let it stop me. I figured a woman should know what a man should look like, and even though I never let it bother me, sometimes I had insecurities. I knew I wanted to be one of the top barbers in my area and with persistence I was only getting better at cutting hair. Plus, I always took pride in my work, and I was willing to work for my place in this industry.

For the first five years or so, I was always trying to prove myself and become better at my craft. I mostly had male clients, but I was open to doing women's hair too. It wasn't long before I realized that I wanted to learn everything and specialize in mastering haircutting—any texture, any length. I wanted to be able to take anyone who walked in the door, and honestly, this is the best thing I ever could have done for my career.

Being able to only do certain textures or certain haircuts definitely limits you on the number of clients you can take. And telling someone you can't do what they are asking for can often leave you feeling unconfident and unprofessional. Unless you really don't like doing a service, I say challenge yourself and learn a little bit of everything. Not only do you increase your professionalism, but you also increase your revenue; trust me, it will all make sense in the end.

As you branch out, you will need to strive to improve your skills. I was always pushing to improve my skills even if I was uncomfortable with the haircut or if the client was skeptical about coming to me. I feel that the uncertainty of the client made me strive to perfect my craft, pay attention to detail, and give each client the haircut they asked for.

Being a barber became an addictive challenge for me, and I realized it was special when I felt a more heightened sense of love for my talent every time I received a compliment. I always did my best to make it a point to never do a bad haircut because I didn't want anyone to say I did it. I suggest as you move throughout your career, you should always take pride in your work and strive to improve your skillset.

<u>The Up, The Down and Full Circle Moments</u>

My down.

After being a barber for five years, I felt very confident in my skills, and I no longer felt I needed to prove myself. I had a healthy amount of clients, and I was dedicated to my profession. I was working at a full service salon and sitting at the front desk. This guy comes in and said he needed a haircut. I said, "I'm available I can take you!"

Hesitantly he asked, "There are no barbers here?"

I said, "I'm a barber," and he didn't say anything. I could tell he didn't want me to cut his hair, so I quickly said, "There's a barbershop across the street if you want to go over there." So, he said okay and left. I felt a little discouraged; this was the first time I experienced this, and although I had a good reputation, none of that mattered if I wasn't even given a chance, but I told myself that that was to be expected and I shook it off.

Three weeks later he came in again and said, "Are you available?" When he got in my chair, he apologized and went on to tell me that the barber across the street keeps cancelling on him, and he likes to get his haircut once a week, so I went on to cut his hair. He became my client for years. I learned a valuable lesson from this, and I'm sure he did too. So, my advice is to never let self-doubt get the best of you, keep going, be consistent, believe in yourself, and don't take anything personally. You just need to work hard, and what will be for you, will always be for you no matter what.

My up.

About 10 years into my career, I was already in the music industry, working with a lot of artists, and because I was completely committed to my career, I made a lot of sacrafices which included some friends and a personal life. I worked every day on call or in the barbershop, so there was no time for rest, and I was always tired, but if you asked me I was living my dream, and at the end of the day, I appreciated it all.

What confirmed it for me was one of the biggest compliments I ever received as a barber. I was attending the grand opening of my friend's boutique called "The Wardrobe Department LA," which is a savvy clothing and lifestyle boutique filled with trendy unique pieces that are handpicked by my amazing friend. Anyhow, she is a stylist for the stars, and among all of her guests, Nas was there. He's a legend in Hip Hop, and I am a fan as well. He was standing near me, so I built up the nerve to say something to him. I said, "Hi, my name is Tracy, nice to meet you. I'm such a fan!"

He said, "I know who you are, nice to meet you!"

I said, "You do?!"

He said, "Yeah, you cut hair, right?"

Surprised, I said "Yes, I do!"

"I know; it's an honor," he said and shook my hand!

I stood there for a minute stunned and thought, Wow! No one will ever believe this! I can't begin to tell you how this made me feel, but it made me realize that I was doing everything that I was supposed to be doing, and all of the long nights, hard times, self-doubts, successes, failures, accomplishments, and sacrifices were all worth it.

Full Circle.

Later in my career, I had an artist who was shooting a music video, and I was there as his barber/groomer and had to groom him throughout the video. There was another artist who was in the video as well who I had just met.

In the first scene of the video, they didn't need a haircut because they needed to be portraying themselves as if they knew each other from when they were both broke and trying to make it. Then in the second scene, they needed to show themselves starting their company and becoming very successful. So, to show continuity of them hustling in the beginning with no haircuts to becoming successful, I had to make sure they both looked clean-cut in the second scene.

I could sense the other artist was nervous about me cutting his hair. He had curly hair with a taper and a scruffy beard, so he definitely needed it all to be cleaned up. He told me he never had a woman cut his hair, but needless to say, he was happy with it and in the end and he wanted me to give his manager my number. About a week later, his manager called me to do a house call for him, I showed up and after a few times he began to be comfortable with me and he would say he was going to make me his personal barber because he liked getting his haircut by a woman, because she knows how a man should look. Pretty ironic if you ask me.

I have had alot of proud moments, and they have all assured me persistence creates success, and you can persevere through any challenges when you are determined to win.

For All My Female Barbers

Yes, this job can be fun and rewarding, but being a female barber in a male-dominated industry is not easy. Most of the time you will feel challenged yet motivated to take this industry on, but along the way, there are also a lot of sacrifices that will be made. It can be bittersweet. You must be professional foremost and confident about your work. Be consistent in your talent, stand up for yourself, and make sure you are always on top of your game. Plus, you have to always be aware and cautious whether you're traveling, doing house calls, or in the shop alone.

Always trust your intuition.

As a woman in this industry, you need to be cautious about your safety and surroundings. You may be the only female in the room at times so make sure you are aware of the company you keep. You will also spend a lot of time by yourself, especially if you are traveling between the shop, house calls, and gigs. This can be dangerous at times, and anything can happen.

I remember one night, close to Christmas, I was out late, working. By the time I got to my car, the parking attendant had left for the night. I got my keys from the front desk and proceeded to leave. I talked on the phone during my hour drive home, parked in my garage, and went to bed. I was awakened by my daughter asking me if I had someone in my truck or if I brought a friend home. I was exhausted and half asleep but quickly realized what she was asking. When I said no, she told me someone is in your truck. I jumped up and ran outside as fast as I could. I was terrified, but I was more angry than I was scared, and before I knew it, I was out there in a rage!

There stood this man I didn't know, holding my shears in his hand, as if they were a weapon! Without hesitating I yelled, "Where are my f*****g clippers!" I had no idea where he came from or how he got in my truck, and he had no idea where he was. I was so mad, fear was not an option, I was about to seriously hurt this guy. I believe he was more scared of me than I was of him. He ultimately told me he thought it was his friend's vehicle, that he had been drinking too much, and he just wanted to sleep it off. I told him I didn't care who he was or where he was about to go, but he was going to get out of there and never come back. He immediately dropped my shears and took off; I never saw him again.

Luckily, this guy seemed harmless, but that could have been anyone in there and the thought that he had access to my home and family throughout the night makes me still feel sick, but it made me realize how blessed I am that we are always protected, and it definitely makes me more cautious when I'm out at night working. Remember, you must always be careful and aware of who you are dealing with, and your surroundings at all times.

But ultimately, whether you are a man or woman, being a barber is such an incredible, fulfilling, authentic, gifted craft and it is truly a blessing to be a part of such a talented industry. Even through all the tough times, challenges, and moments we can feel unnoticed, it should make us stronger, want to be better, want to work harder and strive for bigger goals.

No matter what, when the wins are happening it is important to take the time to live in those great moments; these are milestones, so they need to be recognized. They are most important because they validate the fact that you are making all the right decisions and you are heading in the right direction.

> *We as barbers not only contribute a lot to society with our talents, but we are also part of a powerful significant workforce.*

Chapter Four

The Barbershop.

There is something special about the barbershop and we all can feel it the moment we walk in. And we all know that over the years, both cutting hair and hairstyling have become essential in communities all over the world for both men and women. The barbershop since the beginning of time, was a staple for many neighborhoods all around the world and over time has created its own culture and has also cultivated its own sense of community. The barbershop is not only a place for men to get a fresh haircut, but also a therapeutic space for them to come feel relaxed and share their everyday life experiences.

Hairstylists or hairstyling on the other hand, when it first began, was actually formed from barbering, then eventually as time went on, women began to branch off and create their own space to get done up and to share their stories. Now, barbering is mostly focused only on men's grooming.

Barbers are highly skilled, independent creative people who are very passionate about what they do and express their talents daily by giving the trendiest haircuts and hairstyles they can. They are always raising the bar making barbering one of the most admired professions.

The Hair Industry

People, in general, have become more aware of their appearance and have made it a priority in their weekly budgets and daily regimen to get their hair cut, styled, braided or just get a beard trim as often as needed. Even hair styling products and hair tools (clippers, razors, blow-dryers, etc.) have become a necessity for everyone to maintain looks in between services. Not only is it preferable for some guys to get their hair cut, beard trimmed, or just a shapeup once a week to stay looking fresh all the time, some are even obsessed with shapeups twice a week! It has become necessary for some people to maintain a clean, well-kept look for their job, so their trips to the barbershop are more frequent. This goes to show that appearances are important therefore, so are you!

The fact that both men and women will spend hundreds of thousands of dollars on beauty over a lifetime proves that people are not only serious about how they look and present themselves, but they are also dedicated to feeling great.

With social media being the forefront of our society nowadays, it has definitely proven how we have entered an ever-growing marketplace of consumers. Everyone wants to feel good about their appearance despite the cost and the amount of time they are in the barbershop.

From personal experience, on average, most men will visit the barbershop about every 2–4 weeks for a haircut and beard trim if necessary. Although I can say I have quite a few men that come in once a week for their weekly haircut. And don't be surprised if you have a client come in twice a week, once for just a line-up and the second time for a haircut. These men typically keep their hair shaved down to a zero (almost bald) and like their lineups fresh and clean.

If they like the job you do, they will not have a problem paying you to save them time in the morning to keep them looking fresh. Not only is choosing to cut hair special, but the beauty industry as a whole, is at an all-time high and isn't going anywhere, anytime soon so you have definitely chosen the right profession.

Men not only rely on just looking good to feel good, but they also get haircuts for many important reasons such as interviews, date nights, weekend outings with friends and family, or special occasions like holidays, birthdays, events, or special once-in-a-lifetime moments like weddings.

A haircut can make a huge difference in their lives; it makes a significant change in their confidence and can make a difference in whether or not they get that job they are seeking or that date they are hoping for. So, if you came into this industry to make people feel good, express your talents, and make money, you better believe you will! And, in this ever-changing, on-the-go world, you will constantly be working, changing lives, and making people feel their best every day!

The Barbershop and You

Not only is this a special job because you make a difference in people's lives, but this job also makes an even bigger impact on your life. It feels amazing when you can love doing something so much that you can feel the passion for it from within yourself. It becomes such a major part of your everyday life, that you are constantly thinking about it, and you will even catch yourself looking at people's haircuts and thinking "that's a great haircut!" Or "I know how I can make that a haircut better." Whether you know it or not you are constantly growing and focusing every day on making yourself better. The opportunities for you in this industry are endless. You should automatically feel the job security from the first day you begin, simply because you know that people are always going to want a haircut, and you will always be in demand.

Customer Service

One of the most important aspects of being barber is not only about the amount of money you can make, but also about the customers you service. We all know we can create a generous income for ourselves through barbering and the daily amount of money we can make can add up quickly. $40 haircuts can easily turn into a $2000 week, but it won't be steady if you don't have consistent good customer service.

Clients can be challenging, and we all have a few that don't make it easy for us, but treating the clients who are loyal and respect your time, with the same courtesy will continue to be a returning customer for years to come. Appreciate your clients. Building a business work ethic based around your clients will keep you busy on a regular basis. Customer service should be your number one priority, if you want to be a successful barber.

Here are a few tips for keeping a solid clientele:

*Be on time for appointments.

*Pay attention to detail.

*Give your client your undivided attention for the 30-45 minutes they are in your chair.

*Specialize your haircuts for each client to their needs.

* Let them vent, be consistently genuine, show empathy and be the person they can be comfortable talking to.

We as barbers not only contribute a lot to society with our talents, we are also part of a powerful significant workforce and should be considered essential to the community. We are not only capable of curating a substantial income, we do it with a touch of love.

Besides the service you provide, we all know that barbershops are more than just a place to come and get haircuts. It is a place to come and get your confidence back. A place to come and talk about all things from sports to personal issues. A place to relax after a long day of work. A place to come joke around, talk about endless issues, watch TV or sports events, and in some barbershops, enjoy a beer to start the weekend off. And when the service is great, it's also a place to bring your family and tell your friends about.

Bottom line, the barbershop is a special place for men to look forward to coming to. Most people will come back to you for years and years. You will witness your clients get married, start families, and cross major milestones in their lives. Over time you will cut generations of families, and sadly enough, you may even have some clients pass away. But through it all, you will meet some amazing people that do amazing things; some may even be able to help you out a time or two.

Ultimately, clients are people who share their lives with you, and you may find yourself sharing your life with them as well. As you become close with them over the years, they will feel they can trust and confide in you and look to you for advice. You see, being a barber not only means you cut someone's hair, but you also become your client's confidant, therapist, and in most cases, friend.

Always remember every move you make in your career is strategic to your success.

Chapter Five

Finding the Right Barbershop

Let's note that not all barbershops are the same and finding the perfect barbershop for you to start your career in or make your next move to may not be easy. But let's just say you just graduated; you are an entrepreneur for the first time and you are ready to venture into the real world. You probably feel excited, confident, and scared all at the same time.

Maybe you have a plan all set up and have a place to start your new career. But what if you don't? What if school was all you were focused on, and you haven't thought about what happens after? This can be a little intimidating since school was such a huge part of your life, and you became very accustomed to it. During school, having clientele was a given, and you didn't have to do anything but show up. Although you wanted to do a good job, you weren't expected to because you were a student, and you were still learning. The expectations were already set for you at school, and now you're out on your own into the reality that you are now responsible for everything that happens in your career; this could push that intimidation bar for you a little higher.

Now you have to find a barbershop to work in, and maybe you are having some doubts as to if you have gained enough knowledge to hold your ground in this highly demanding world of people that hold their looks and appearance to a very high standard.

The first thing you need to know is: You've got this! Have faith in yourself, don't set limitations, keep the mentality of taking pride in your work with every single haircut for every client, and get ready to start living your purpose!

Before we get started with looking for a shop for you to start your new profession in, or even if you have been in this industry for a while and you are looking for a new place to work, this chapter can help you with deciding on a new place to take your talents.

Always remember that no matter how long you have been in this industry, you want to make sure every move you make in your career is strategic to your success. Always make sure it will be somewhere that allows you to strengthen your skills, supports your vision and motivates you to do more.

Now, let's discuss an important reason to space out your career correctly and really pay attention to where you decide to work because these decisions matter towards the success of your future. Each move you make throughout your career has to be a part of your plan to become a successful entrepreneur. As you are choosing shops to work in, make these decisions based on becoming a better person, growing with your purpose, and becoming a better barber. Always push yourself and level up.

Cut Everyone!

You want to make sure you will be able to grow more with each move you make, so I feel one of the most important tasks you could do in this industry, is to learn how to cut different ethnicities. Also, familiarize yourself with different textures and styles.

You will need to put yourself in different environments throughout your cutting career and learn as much as you can to enhance your growth. You will need to open your mind to all challenges because this will be your biggest asset and at the right moment could catapult your career to multiple levels.

I know this can be difficult at times and sometimes even discouraging; it will take a lot of determination, courage, and confidence to keep taking clients you are not familiar with and doing haircuts you have never done. Every haircut takes practice to master, so you have to be up for the challenge if you want to elevate your skills. But I say educate yourself with classes, watch other barbers or stylists, take your time, think about your process, stay focused, and always look to improve and sharpen your techniques any chance you get.

So, here are a few reasons you should take the time to learn to do different ethnicities.

First and foremost, learning different ethnicities is crucial to your revenue and most of all, your confidence in cutting hair. To do so takes a great deal of time and experience but is worth every minute. Your goal should be, to be able to take any client who walks in the door. Or better yet, if your goal is to be in the entertainment industry, being a versatile barber is a major plus and will open the door to many jobs.

Learning to perfect your craft should be an everyday goal that will eventually be what separates you from all the other barbers.

Here are just a few other reasons why throughout your career you will need to be versatile.

1. For the barbershop, it speaks volumes to be able to take anyone who walks in the door and wants a haircut. It shows that the establishment is professional and experienced. It allows you to potentially gain a new client just from being able to confidently say, "Yes, I can take you. Have a seat!"

2. For you, it will allow your confidence level to be at its highest. It will allow you to move in a more consistent, organized manner which increases your speed between each client, enabling you to be more efficient with your haircuts, which equals more revenue.

3. It will also allow you to not be hesitant to try new styles on clients, allowing you to be more creative with the look your client is trying to achieve. Overall, it will give you a great understanding and visualization of haircutting and styling on anyone.

4. And, if you are looking to be in the entertainment industry, this talent can

increase the number of jobs you can say yes to, thereby, increasing your revenue as well. Being versatile can create a lot of opportunities in this industry; you just have to be confident in yourself and your talent. We will talk more about the pressures of being on the barber/male grooming side of the entertainment business later in the book.

Finding a Shop

With these goals in mind, let's start the journey and look for a new barbershop to work in. Go around to a couple of shops in your area and start talking to the owners. Get an idea of how their shop is ran; take a look around at the environment and see if you can visualize yourself working there.

There are a lot of questions you need to think through before you decide on a shop to work in. Aside from working someplace where you can gain knowledge and grow, you want to find a shop you and your clients will enjoy and have memorable experiences at.

Let's look at some significant questions to consider when choosing a shop to work at:

Shop Business:
Services, Booth Rent or Commission and Barbershop or Full-Service?

* Questions for consideration:
* How much are their services? (Haircuts, shaves, color, etc.)
* Are they booth rent or commission?
* Will the owner offer you commission until you build your clientele?
* Is this a Barbershop or Full-Service Salon?

Services

These questions are probably going to be the most important questions for you as they are going to play a major role in figuring out if this establishment is for you or not. These questions go hand in hand, and depending on the state and area you live in, it will make a significant difference in what their rates are and what services they are offering.

A lot of high-end salons in upper-class areas offering full services charge higher rates for their services. Therefore, if you chose to work at one of these shops you could have the opportunity to make a lot of money, and I'm positive you would receive some good tips as well. This is a great option for barbers who are already fluent in every service and can offer quality work. Take note, the booth rent at these shops tend to be very high, so if you choose to work at a place like this, you will have to make sure you are ready to take on this responsibility. I recommend that if you have any doubts or concerns about covering the cost of boothrent or the amount of responsibility you can handle, you can always offer to start as an assistant to the stylists or barbers and get used to the environment, clients, and services first.

This is often the best route to go because you could learn a lot and apply those techniques to your catalog of skills once you decide to become a full-time barber there. This is also a smart way to go if you want to jump right into a high-end salon. I mean, yes, being an assistant may take some invested time, but you're learning capabilities are endless.

If I haven't learned anything else in the hair industry, it's that no matter what happens, where you go, or how many shops you decide to work in, nobody can take away anything you have learned along the way. And wherever you go, your knowledge will always go with you. This is where you have taken the time to invest in yourself.

Booth rent

Typically, if you are paying booth rent, you are your own business, so you will need to apply for your business license down at your local city hall or online. It is not a long process, but you will be filling out a questionnaire with pertinent information associated with your new business.

It will be a different price, depending on your city, but it shouldn't be too expensive. They typically go off your projected annual income; for instance, if you are brand new and have no idea what you are going to make annually, you could keep your projection low, let's say $20,000, and your license fee will be based on that amount. In California I paid about $34 for the initial fee, so be prepared to answer that question. Along with completing the questionnaire, you will also need to have your barber license available to verify and to fill out the required information.

Also, think about what you will want your business to be called because that is what will be printed on your business license, business bank account, and business cards (yes, you will want to make those), and you will also use it on your taxes. In the next chapter, we will discuss taxes and other considerations for being self-employed.

Renting your booth means it's your space, so you will charge what you want for your services. You will want to check on the rates in the shop you are thinking of working at and the going rates in the area so you can stay competitive.

Also, when charging for services, make sure you are planning to stay consistent with your rates for every client, and when you are ready for a price increase give your customers a specific date well ahead of time when the price will change, so they are prepared.

Renting your booth also requires you to be responsible for buying your own tools, products, and anything else you will need.

You will most likely have a key to the shop because you will be creating your own schedule. If you want to take a day or two off, you can, or if you want to take a vacation, you can. Sounds great, huh? Just remember that usually booth rent is due every week and the day is at the owner's discretion, and whether you decide to take a day or a week off, you still have to pay your rent on the day it is due.

But on the positive side, it is nice to have the freedom to make as much money as you want and have no one to answer to when it comes to your schedule or when you want or need to take a day off. The independence of it is priceless. In my area booth rent runs about $275 a week; that can range from $1,100–$1,375 a month. This adds up and does not include products, equipment, or anything else you may need, or any personal bills you may have.

I suggest you have a steady clientele before you commit to booth rent. Most places that are booth rent only will give you a three-month grace period of either a discounted rate or they will do commission with you, and hopefully, after the three months are over, you would have built up your clientele enough to afford your booth rent.

I suggest if you take this route, plan on being there all day, and every day that the shop is open, to take advantage of all the walk-ins and to also be available for the clients you do have.

Commission

Commission means the owner will take a certain percentage out of the money you make for the day. You will be able to keep your tips, of course, but the money you make on services will be split. The amount of commission depends on the shop owner and the going rate of the area. I've seen some do 60/40 (60 percent to you and 40 percent to the owner), which is quite high, but mostly I've seen 65/35. If you find somewhere that will do 70/30, that is ideal. Some owners like to be creative and create their own incentives for their barbers and do flexible commission. This approach can be very successful with a good owner.

If you are on commission, you will most likely be on a schedule at the shop. Most owners like for you to be there all the time depending on their business hours unless you have worked out a schedule with them. This is because the more you are there and able to take walk-ins, the more they are making money, and so are you. This will also allow you to build your clientele.

The prices for the services the shop offers are usually set by the owner, so before you decide to work there, make sure you agree with the prices they charge for services, and they are competitive for the area.

The shop owner should supply you with basic products like shampoo, Clippercide, Quats (disinfectant), hair products, and shaving cream, but with my experience, you may want to buy most of your products and supplies especially once you find ones you like.

Hopefully, if you are on commission or booth rent, the owner provides the shop with a receptionist and towel service, so you have help and clean towels available when you need them. I think, after the pandemic of 2020, towel service should be mandatory along with strict rules for sanitation for clients and staff, but that's just my opinion.

Having a receptionist is up to the discretion of the owner, but it is very helpful and allows you to be able to focus on your clients and services without distractions. Receptionists also help keep the shop clean, sweep after each haircut, answer phones, and book appointments for you and other barbers when clients call. They will also be the first one to welcome the client when they walk in the door or make small trips like lunch, and even though you may have to give them a gratuity tip at the end of the day, it is worth it! Having a good receptionist makes it so convenient on busy days.

Being on commission, the owner will not typically give you a key to the shop, but I have seen some that do, but only after you have been there for some time and have shown signs that you are going to work there permanently.

On commission, you can take days off and vacations, but these need to be discussed with the owner because if you're not there to take clients, they don't make any money and neither do you.

Commission is a great way to start if you don't have any clientele because if the day/week is slow, you don't make any money, but you also don't owe booth rent at the end of a slow week, either.

Tip: If you don't have clientele, and the shop you want to work at offers both commission and booth rent, I recommend you start on commission. Once you have reached a consistent clientele, you will be making more money, so at that point, the percentage you will be paying the owner on your commission will outweigh the amount you would be paying for booth rent. That is when you would want to talk to the owner and switch to booth rent.

Barbershop or Full-Service Salon

So, working at a full-service salon is exactly how it sounds –full service; they are salons that offer everything from men and women's haircare, skincare, to possibly nails as well.

The goal of a full-service salon is to be a one-stop-shop, and it is ideal for an owner to have highly skilled, motivated, consistent, multitalented people working there. This is not only beneficial for the owner, but it's also extremely beneficial for you because clients will be happy, and business will be thriving within the shop as well. It's also somewhere the whole family can go and be serviced, so referrals to friends and family are almost guaranteed.

If you can find a place like this where there are different cultures and talents, you may have found the perfect place. Having a place that serves everybody means there are no limits to the amount of money you can make because everyone is welcome. It doesn't necessarily have to be in high-end areas either. I worked in a full-service Salon for about four years. I loved it there. There were so many different cultures and personalities. The employees ranged from hairstylists, colorists, barbers, estheticians, massage therapists, and a nail tech. It was really fun and a great experience, everyone was nice, hardworking, and talented.

We all got along, and we all specialized in different services and taught each other so much. We had so many different types of clients coming in there, and anytime they needed a different service, we would just recommend them to one of our coworkers. Since the client was so familiar with everyone, it was always very easy and convenient for them, and it kept all the business in house. Full-Service salons are not just in wealthy areas; they are all over.

Typically, in a barbershop, the booth rent is lower than a full-service salon, and it generally only specializes in men's haircuts and shaves. But now that men are looking to be a little more pampered and groomed, they are open to going to a full-service salon, or the now super trendy shops that not only cater to men's haircare, but they also offer a variety of services from haircuts, shaves, haircolor, manicures, pedicures, and facials, just for men.

These type of trendy man caves are a more exclusive place and prices for services will most likely be higher, and more than likely, so will your booth rent. However, it may be just what you're looking for, you just have to really think about your goals and what type of environment you want to work in.

Whatever you choose, make sure it lines up with your goals and you have room to grow.

If you are a barber just coming out of school and you are unsure, I recommend starting at a traditional barbershop to get your cutting techniques and skills to the level you want them to be. Get a feel for how the business is ran, build some clientele, and when you feel you have reached your full potential and you're ready for change, do some research, plan your next move, and move on.

Remember, if you do this the right way, growth will always be respected.

Still Undecided?
If you still haven't decided if you want to work at a barbershop or a full-service salon, let's talk a little bit more about it now because this is something to consider.

Earlier I suggested that if you are a newly licensed barber, starting in a barbershop is the best route to go. Most barbers I knew went to a barbershop after they finished school; after all, that was the vision they had when they decided they wanted to cut hair. A lot of inspiration comes out of the barbershop, and most people that decide to become a barber, start there, which is a good idea because you can really get a true feel of how a barbershop operates, learn alot of tricks of the trade and be inspired at the same time.

You will also be introduced to hair shows and barber battles because when those type of events are going on; barbershops are the first to know. These events are always fun and super inspiring, you will learn a lot and have an opportunity to pick up new tools and products. We will go more in depth with hair shows later in the book.

You will also have other barbers in the shop that you can learn great cutting techniques from to add to your own. You will also be able to see what products or tools they are using that you may like, ask all the questions you want, and I'm sure at some point that you will need to know how to work on your tools like adjusting your clippers, such as zero gapping, and you can get help on learning that as well. There are so many things to anticipate and be excited about when you work in a barbershop for the first time.

When I first got out of school, I worked at a barbershop. I loved working there and I learned a lot. I remember when I wasn't' able to do the greatest fade, and the barbers would make fun of me after the client left. And even though I laughed it off, it really made me a better barber. It made me pay attention to detail and use my mirror to see where my weight lines were in my haircuts so I could make my fades better. I remember being excited to learn different techniques and incorporate them into my cutting style. Over the four years I worked there, I learned so much and made some great friends. I talk more about the type of barbershops I worked in and why later on in the book.

Overall, being in a barbershop straight out of school can bring many great experiences and a lot of fun memories. And, if you find a busy one, you can look forward to a lot of new clients looking for a barber they can not only talk to, laugh with, and confide in every two weeks, but one they can trust with their appearance.

Now, there are benefits of working in a full-service salon as well. Because they serve both men and women, this is ideal for a cosmetologist, but if you are a barber and you are interested in cosmetology too, you could look into working at a full-service salon and look forward to learning different services such as cutting, styling long hair, and more. There will be a lot of stylists there doing color, so you could watch, ask questions, and possibly be able to work with haircolor on some of your clients and not be intimidated because you have a lot of great help right there.

Sometimes in a barbershop, men won't ask for color unless they are concerned with gray hair coming in, and even then, sometimes they're a little hesitant or won't even ask at all, you can obviously mention and introduce color services but if they were in a full-service salon, they will see color being done often and be more apt to inquire—if not just to cover their gray, but to possibly change their natural haircolor to something trendy.

If you are in a barbershop already and you are considering going to a full-service salon or just want to offer more services, I recommend taking the time to take some hands-on classes outside of your shop, there are tons of classes that are put on by your favorite companies from clipper cutting, haircutting, haircoloring, braiding, hair extensions, building your business, and more. There are also tons of videos online to grab ideas from or learn from co-workers to get experience in all types of services.

Education is key to opportunity and is the greatest thing you can do for your career. You never know when you will be asked if you can do a service, and you don't want to have to say no from lack of experience.

The more you know, the more money you can make, it's that simple.

If you plan on taking your talents to the entertainment industry, you will want to be well rounded in all aspects of hair. We will discuss the entertainment industry later in the book as well.

Shop Scene:
Location, Success, Days and Hours

Questions for consideration:

* Is the location close to home?
* Is the location in a great area for customers to walk in?
* Is the shop busy at the moment?

Location and Success

One thing you want to consider is your commute time. Is the shop busy enough for you to make the commute worth it? If the shop is reputable, in a busy area, and close to home, perfect! If not, look around while you are in the shop and see if it's busy with clients or if the barbers are just sitting around. Not to say the shop will be busy all the time, but before you ultimately decide to work there, you should visit a couple of times possibly on a Monday or Tuesday, and then again on a busy Friday. Regardless, depending on the day of the week, clients should be coming in and out or calling to schedule appointments. Make sure of this because building clientele for yourself can be difficult, and it may also take some time.

Ultimately, this will let you know if making the commitment there is worth it, and it will make a huge difference in your decision to work there. Ideally, you want your workplace to be close to you, accessible as possible and be in a great location to ensure a high walk-in of customers. This will not only help you build clientele but will also put consistent money in your pocket.

Shop Environment
First impression, Are barbers friendly, Customer Service, Longevity and Quality Work.

Questions for consideration:

* What first impression did you get when you walked in?
* Do the other barbers seem friendly? Do they have good customer service?
* Does the shop do quality work?
* Are there barbers or stylists that have been there for a long time?

First Impression

So, when you go into a barbershop for the first time looking to work there, you want to pay attention to the energy and vibe of the shop as soon as you walk in. Pay attention to how it makes you feel. Does someone greet you as soon as you walk in? Is it clean? Is there a TV or music playing in the background setting the mood? It's important to notice all of these things. It should have some liveliness, a feel-good flow, great conversation, and a welcoming feeling. This will be the same experience your clients or a new client will have when they walk in too. You only get one chance at this, so don't forget to pay attention.

Are the Barbers Friendly?

Observe if the barbers seem friendly or not when you inquire about working there. Were they willing to help you? Are they having conversations with their clients? Do the clients look happy? Remember, you will be working side by side with these same people, and it can be hard if you have a co-worker that isn't so nice and doesn't have a good attitude towards others.

This is important especially since you will be spending a significant amount of time together in a rather small space. If they are rude, this may not be the place for you. These are not the type of co-workers you want to be next to all day. You need to work with other barbers that you can look to for help, guidance, or inspiration when you need it. As I mentioned before, the first impression is the most important and it speaks volumes about a place.

Customer Service

If an environment feels good to you it will also feel good to your clients. Customer service and a good haircut go hand in hand. If someone gets a good haircut but bad vibes every time they go into a shop, they may not come back at some point. And you can forget them recommending for someone else to come there. There are a lot of competitive shops and great barbers out there ready to take on a new client, so make sure your clients are comfortable and enjoy your barbershop experience to keep them coming back. Even if you didn't give them the exact haircut they wanted, but the environment was pleasant, they will most likely return to give you another try.

When someone goes somewhere for the first time and has a great experience, they may tell a few people that day, but if someone has a bad experience, they will tell everybody they encounter how bad their experience was. Do not be that bad experience.

I have known barbers who didn't really care if the client was satisfied or if they would become a returning customer. I have also heard people complain about bad haircuts or that their barber was always cancelling or wasn't even showing up for appointments. I knew a barber that would hurry up to get the client out and skip on certain things, like not cutting the hair on the back of someone's neck once the cape was undone.

These types of bad habits will never keep a client coming back no matter how skilled you are. I learned that reliability and attention to detail are essential. Every customer not only wants your complete attention while they are with you, but they also always want a consistently good haircut.

Quality Work

This brings us to quality haircuts. If you can, see if the barbers are doing a good job on their clients. You might want to stay around to see a few leave.

It's important to notice this for a couple of reasons. One, if the client is leaving with a bad haircut, people that are outside don't know it wasn't you that did the service; they don't know who it was, so they will attribute it to the entire shop, and most likely won't go there for a haircut.

Whatever comes out of your shop in terms of the quality of the work and customer service makes a difference in everyone's pockets, and whether clients will come back or refer other people they know. This affects everyone in the shop, including you. I have had clients tell me when they are going somewhere new for a haircut, they will sit and watch customers come out before they decided if they want to go in.

So, a talented staff is a quality your new shop must have, or it may have to be a deal-breaker for you. Plus, if you see great work coming out of there, you know that you will be able to join a talented team that you can build with.

Longevity

When you have your first conversation with the owner ask if there are any barbers that have been there for a long time. This not only shows you longevity in the shop, but it says a lot about the owner and their business tactics. Plus, there's nothing like having an experienced, friendly co-worker that can possibly share their knowledge and skills with you.

In the end ask yourself if this is a place you can grow. Remember, people can take everything from you, but they can't take away your experience and what you have learned through the years. What you learn along the way is what will make you an amazing barber. So having people around that are grounded and have a good business ethic will help you in creating good customer service and longevity for yourself as well.

Experience will always make you irreplaceable.

Shop Expectations
Cleanliness/Regulations and Staying Prepared

Questions to consider:

1. Is the Shop Clean?
2. Are you prepared for State Board?

Every shop has expectations it must meet based on the State Board requirements. So, as you check out the shop, you will want to make sure it is clean, and meets the states rules and regulations. You may not know what all these regulations are, but if the shop is clean and licenses are noticeable, these are good signs that the shop is up to standards.

Cleanliness/Regulations

Now, ask yourself if this is a place you would come to get your hair cut? Is the shop clean and well maintained? Does this shop have a receptionist to help maintain the shop's cleanliness; if not, do they have a cleaning crew that comes in on the weekends to clean so it is ready to go for the next week? There's a lot involved with finding the perfect place, but it's important to make sure the shop is up to standards.

It may seem like a lot to go through but if you nail everything you are looking for in a shop, you will have fewer problems later.

The cleanliness of the shop is high on the list of priorities. If State Board decides to pay an unexpected visit, you don't want them to find anything wrong and start issuing fines. If they find a lot of problems, not only will this be expensive, but they will also come back often to make sure the shop is up to standards.

Staying Prepared

There is a lot to know, and the standards of State Board are high. But if you are a barber, and not a shop owner, only a portion of these apply to you, so if you just keep up with the basics of regular sanitation you should be fine.

Generally, the owner will be good at staying up on these codes and standards because the fines are steep. However, the owner may be on you to keep up with your own sanitation requirements as well because if State Board walks in and fines you, the same amount you are fined, the owner will be fined as well. This will be a double fine, so it is very important to keep up with keeping your area clean, following sanitation rules, and making sure your station and things are labeled correctly.

Fines start at one hundred dollars. So, when you're checking out a barbershop, make sure it appears to value these regulations. You can tell quickly by looking around and noticing if you see any labels marked soiled or clean, if the shop's business license is hanging in a noticeable area, and if the barbers have their licenses hanging in clear view as well. All of these should be pretty noticeable.

When you start at a shop, follow these key tips to make sure you and your area are prepared:

1. Have your license/business license visibly displayed at your station.
2. Label all of your belongings appropriately (Soiled, clean, water, etc.).
3. Have clean Barbicide (disinfectant solution) in an appropriate jar for your soiled implements (change frequently).
4. Keep your area clean (no Sanex strips on the floor; you will be fined).
5. Have a proper disposal container (make sure it is labeled) for your razors and make sure none are exposed; this is a big fine!

I recommend you make these tips second nature so you can keep up with it easily. I learned first hand how important it is to know your sanitation rules on implements and why to follow State Board rules to the best of your ability.

The first barbershop I worked in, State Board paid us an unexpected visit. I was fairly new, and the owner had removed the business license that day to go take care of some business. Right when State Board came in, he walked directly to me and asked me what procedure I used to sanitize my implements and tools, so I told him exactly what I learned in school; he took note and walked away.

Then he recognized that the business license for the shop wasn't posted and gave me a $1,500 fine for it because he said it appeared I was working in an unlicensed establishment. I was also the only one fined, so when I asked why, he said it was because I was in the first chair. I tried to explain why the license wasn't there, and he said to have the owner handle it. So, I called State Board the next day and they talked to the owner. I had to fax a copy of the business license, but luckily, they approved it and dismissed the fine. Whew! State Board does not have the friendliest staff and they can be very intimidating and harsh, so make sure you cover your end, and you know and follow all standards and procedures.

Lighting, Station Standards, Fresh Towels and Reviews

Questions for your consideration:

* Is the lighting good?
* Does your station meet your standards with enough space and mats to stand on while working?
* Do they have a towel service?
* What is the shop's Yelp reviews and ratings?

Good Lighting

An important thing to look for in your potential new workplace is if the lighting is adequate. Your shop needs to be well lit. Appropriate lighting is very, very important. This is going to help your haircuts look their best. The wrong lightbulbs can make a huge difference in the time it takes for you to finish your haircuts efficiently and how good your haircuts end up looking as well.

When the lighting is correct, you will be able to see where the weight is in your fades and avoid seeing shadows. With inadequate lighting, even if you use your mirror to see where weight lines are in your haircuts, you will have dark shadowed areas, making it very hard to complete the haircut.

The worst part of not being able to see accurately is you will be straining your eyes, moving slowly to avoid mistakes, and ultimately taking longer for you to finish. Also, when you are finished and they get up, you will look at the haircut and notice areas that need to be touched up again, but at this point, it's too late.

Typically, shops will have light panels on the ceiling and a light over each station. Ultimately, it is best to use an LED lightbulb;

these tend to give the best accurate light we need.

Pro Tip: I suggest you practice not looking in the mirror to blend your haircuts so you're not relying on it and are prepared when you don't have it. Learn to see your weight lines without one. Because if you decide to do house calls or work in entertainment, you will not always have accurate lighting or a mirror to depend on.

My tip is, if you are on the go and you are having a hard time seeing, use a headlight that has a LED lightbulb. This is a tool I rely on when I'm on the move and I have minimal light and no mirror. It does take some practice to learn how to not use your mirror, but you will get good at, so start now.

Station Standards

Something else to consider is if the stations have enough space for you and your equipment. There are a lot of different types of stations that the owner could choose from. Some shops have smaller stations so they can have more barbers, so the amount of space you might end up having may be tight. So, if you notice that there are a lot of stations in a small shop, make sure you will have enough space and think about how comfortable you and your clients will be.

You can always purchase a roll-a-bout to use for additional space, but you will need room either next to or underneath your station to store it. Also, make sure that there is space for products, tools, blow dryer, plus any extra equipment.

Hopefully, the owner has an extra storage unit available for you to use so you can have an additional area to store things you don't use all the time; plus, this will also give you some extra space for your personal belongings.

Another very important aspect of your potential workplace is making sure you have a mat around your chair to support your legs and feet while you are working. This may not sound important, but after a long day it is because you will be working long hours and standing for most of the day, so these mats will help your legs, feet, and back from aching. If you don't have a mat at your station, and you're on commission you can request that the owner supply you with one; however, if you are booth rent, you may have to purchase your own. But the upside of getting your own is you can purchase one you like, and if you ever leave, you can take it with you.

Fresh Towels

Of course, you are going to be expected to keep your area, tools and implements clean, but towels are going to be an ongoing priority. If you can find a shop that has towel service, that would be the best. Not all of them do because it is more of a privilege than a necessity. It used to be that a lot of shops preferred to have a washer and dryer in the shop instead of towel service to save some money, and I'm not just talking about mom-and-pop shops. I've seen major franchises have them as well and it would be part of the receptionist's job to fold and keep them stocked.

It is nice to find an owner who cares enough to have fresh, clean towels every week delivered from a professional towel company; hopefully it becomes standard for all owners to supply fresh towels for the barbershop.

Yelp Reviews

Last but not least, go on Yelp to help you find a few places to visit. Look at the ratings and read the reviews to help you find out what the good aspects of the shop are and what problems they may be having.

You can definitely tell who has the best customer service and the worst, who does great work and who doesn't, and you may also be able to find out if people have complaints about the owner or if they are great and amazing at solving issues. Keep in mind, potential clients use this tool for the same reasons, so you want to make sure you bring your A-game all the time when you are at work.

Hopefully, this information helps you pick the perfect place to start or continue your journey. I have seen quite a few barbershops where rules and regulations are nonexistent, and there is little respect for the business and clients, which is very unprofessional. The owners of these shops ultimately lack good leadership and communication skills. So, these are the types of shops you want to avoid.

They should have good systems in place for scheduling clients, receiving payment, and for the barbers to pay their commission or booth rent.

There must be a lot of respect between the barbers and the owner. The shop as a whole needs to understand proper customer service and want to be successful for a shop to flow, have happy barbers, and in turn, have happy returning customers.

Finding the perfect shop for you may take a little time, research, and consideration, but it will be worth it. It may be a good idea for you to finish reading this book, take some notes, think carefully about what you expect from the shop you want to work at, and then call around to the barbershops or full-service salons you are considering and narrow it down to your top five places, then go in and talk to the owners. Good luck—you'll do great!

My Experiences

When I graduated, I didn't have a plan. All I knew is I wanted to cut hair, but I had no idea what shop I wanted to work at, so I just started going around to a few places. Yelp was not invented at that time, but there were a few barbershops in the area that were popular.

At the first location, I ran into an old high school friend of mine, and ironically, he was a barber too! When I asked him how the shop was, he told me I wouldn't want to work there because there were a lot of barbers there already and they were struggling for walk-ins. He said that it might be hard for me to get new clients coming straight out of school. So, he recommended me to another shop, not too far away that was fairly new and had more space available. I went and talked to the owners, and this ultimately ended up being my first barbershop.

This was a nice urban barbershop with a modern feel in a suburban area. This shop mainly had barbers, but there were a couple of stylists there as well, so I was able to take women clients as well as men. It was such a great experience, and I learned a lot! I mastered my fades, tapers, lineups, did texturizers, designs, short hair on women, press n curls, flatirons, and learned how to take weaves out.

The owner was a barber and gifted me with my first pair of Andis Master Clippers. I loved those clippers; they meant a lot to me. It didn't take long for me to realize how special they were; I became infatuated with those clippers and mastered them. I knew how to take them apart and put them back together. My love for this brand fueled my career. To this day, their tools are amazing and are still my favorite, hands down. I actually ended up working for them some years down the line. (I discuss this later in the book.)

But I never put a limit on what I could learn, and I'm not really sure I knew it then, but that became a very important part of my career. I was just operating off passion, but this is why I'm sharing it with you now, so you can take advantage of all the opportunities you get to excel in learning everything you can and carry it with you. You will not regret it, I promise!

Although the first shop I worked at was memorable and so much fun, after 4 years it was time for me to go. I realized that I needed more experience and I had reached my limit there.

My next location was a local Supercuts. Supercuts is a franchise with over 2,600 locations across the US. Unfortunately, they aren't known for their great haircuts, but they will get you in at a moment's notice with no appointment necessary. They encourage you to complete haircuts in 20 minutes to receive a commission bonus, but they also offer benefits, which was great because when you are an entrepreneur in a regular barbershop, you are on your own when it comes to any type of benefits. They also offer a lot of training for their employees. I appreciated the training because it did enhance my speed, and I was able to apply their technique to my own, which really set a base for where I start my haircuts, even til this day.

Remember, even if you take one lesson or technique you learned from educational classes, training, or someone, you will have it forever and it will always make you better and enhance your craft.

However, being there I did notice that the stylists are mostly just there for the benefits, so they lack the passion for cutting hair and most of them treat the job like "just a job." Some are in school for another career, so they aren't interested in building a clientele; they are just working part time, trying to make ends meet.

For me, however, I took pride in my work and wanted all my haircuts to look good. I never wanted anyone to say that I did a bad haircut, and if you're serious about this profession neither should you. Not to mention, I planned on having my clients follow me, so customer service and satisfaction meant a lot to me.

Needless to say, I hardly ever made my commission bonus because I took my time and made sure my clients were happy. However, I quickly became a manager, which I enjoyed because my training became more involved, and I got the chance to learn the business and retail side of running a franchise salon. I also got a feel of how it would be to run my own shop and be in charge of employees. At times it was stressful if I had to fix an employee's haircut, but ultimately it improved my skills and allowed me the experience of customer service. Overall, Supercuts was a great experience because I learned how to cut a lot of different ethnicities and textures since different types of people came there for haircuts.

Pro Tip: While you are in school and making mistakes, take the time to learn how to fix them. Start taking the time to think through the haircut and figure out what it will take to fix it. If someone else messes up a haircut, offer to help fix it; eventually, you will get good at it. Remember, if you learn how to fix haircuts, you'll learn not to make mistakes, and if you do, you will be able to fix them.

My next location was a full-service hair salon that was mostly hairdressers, except for one barber. This salon was all different ethnicities: White, Filipino, Black, and Hispanic, with an Italian owner. This place was great! I love a place with a variety of people. We had a great flow of clientele from all ethnicities come in that shop and we had very experienced stylists and barbers. I built up a large clientele, developed a lot of confidence, became fluent in haircolor, and learned a lot about styling hair. I stayed there for a couple of years until the owner decided to sell the shop.

Right before he closed the shop, my co-worker, who was a really good friend of mine, said she was going to buy a salon right down the street and asked if I wanted to come. I did and it was just the two of us until some of the other stylists came a couple of weeks later, and we eventually got a few more stylists as well.

I helped my friend out a lot to get the shop up and running, and I ultimately learned a lot about opening a salon from scratch. I watched it grow over the years and had a lot of great memories there. The one thing I took from that experience is not to open a shop of your own until you know you are ready to dedicate your life to it. It takes an enormous amount of dedication, passion, and hard work to run a successful shop.

I also took some of my biggest steps there and grew so much in the eight years the shop was open. It was in that shop where I made the important decision to focus on myself and put all my energy into me and follow my heart.

At this point in my career, I had a lot of loyal clients and the confidence that I was a great barber and could take anyone who walked in the door.

So ultimately, it was at this shop that I decided to build my portfolio, get more involved with hair shows with Andis and I went to work at a barbershop in LA for a short period of time to ultimately pursue what was my idea of being a Topbarber in the entertainment industry.

After the owner closed the shop, I decided to only do my closest customers from there at my home and focus on my LA clients because I was starting to get really busy.

After a year of being out of the shop, I decided to look for another local barbershop because I missed the environment and the culture. I love the feel of the barbershop and how it keeps me fluent with my haircuts and up to date with current hair and tool trends. But I wanted to find a place my clients would be happy to go to and a shop for me to be in a couple of days a week in between my LA gigs. I found this wonderful shop near my house that has an amazing owner that I love and a great family environment. I really got lucky, and I feel blessed to still be there today.

Along with choosing shops that were either a good fit for me or I knew I could increase my skillset; I made sure each move had a purpose and each place had meaning. My intention with every move was to grow my clientele and expand my expertise. I also made sure throughout my entire career I attended classes, hairshows and events that were going on to help me network and stay on top of trends; the goal was to become as great as I could be.

I hope my journey shows that you can achieve growth with every move you make throughout your career. Allow this journey to be rewarding for both you and your clients. You want to work comfortably in an inspiring environment, make consistent money, and focus on what's important for your business and your clients. Once you start to establish a great flow of clientele, you can start thinking of what you want to create next in this amazing career.

The goal of it all is to invest in yourself and create your own success. Good luck in your journey!

> *...the goal is to grow as a person, be successful, protect yourself and your family, and live comfortably from a business you not only have your heart invested in but that you have built from your passion.*

Chapter Six

Being

Self-Employed

Being in the hair industry is not like a normal job or career, and I admit I didn't think about anything but cutting hair when I started in this industry. I was young and like most of you, all I was focused on was cutting hair and being the best at it. I knew a little about what it was like to have a regular job, but I had no idea of the importance of having benefits and protection for myself and my future. When I started cutting hair, I didn't even realize that I was actually in business for myself and didn't know what it meant to be an entrepreneur or self-employed, all I thought about was making money.

Being self-employed comes with a lot of responsibility and you really have to take the time to protect yourself in every way!

The last thing you want is for something unexpected to happen to you or your family that causes you to wonder- what you are going to do now and how you will you make it through these times.

Dealing with an emotional tragedy can easily escalate to another level when it becomes financial too. When you are an adult and self-employed, you are now responsible for yourself, your family, and your future. Do not wait until it is too late!

In this business you don't have paid family leave, sick time, or vacation time like you would if you were employed by a company for a few years. So then what do you do when you get sick or need to take some time off? This is why you have to be prepared for these times. Part of being your own boss is making sure you are taking care of yourself for the times you need it the most and also for your future.

This might seem like a lot to think about, but I promise it will be the best decision you could make for yourself. After all, while I was writing this book during 2020, we—meaning me, you, and the entire world—were going through a pandemic, a virus that made it impossible for us to work safely, and the world as we knew it instantly changed. This is something I don't think any of us saw coming.

What did you do when this began? Did you have money saved? Did you panic not knowing what you were going to do next? Did you sacrifice your health and the health of the people around you and continue to work? Did you receive your stimulus money from the government?

As you can see this was something so unexpected that it's been hard for everyone, even for the people who were somewhat prepared and had some money saved. This was a very sad time for a lot of small businesses and for a lot of financially unprepared people. Barbershops were closed down twice, and some will never reopen. These were very unforeseen times. Everybody was so unsure about everything and basically living day to day, trying to figure out what was going to happen next.

These topics we will cover now will help you protect yourself and help you feel a little better prepared if something like this happens again.

Building Your Credit

Before I get into all the things that are important for us to have as self-employed bosses, I have to tell you, as a person who has made mistakes, and has learned the hard way, the very first thing I would do is make sure you take the time to learn what your credit score is and work on making it a 720 or higher.

If you don't know what it is or maybe you don't have any credit, take the time to learn; go into your bank, talk to a financial advisor, and ask how you can build your credit and what is the best route for you to take to reach your goal.

Having good credit is not about having a bunch of credit cards. It's about having leverage. It's about having options when you need them most. So, if you don't know anything about credit, how to have good credit, or how to keep it, please do some research and more importantly talk to a professional.

If your credit is not great, find out what is on your credit report that is making it go down, prioritize it, and work on resolving the debt. Credit repair companies can help you, or you can research and fix it yourself.

You cannot survive these days without good credit, and you don't want to get into a position where you need it and don't have it because it can cause major setbacks. And honestly, who has time nowadays to stand still or go backward?

Credit is something that definitely takes time. No matter if you are just starting to build credit or have a credit score you need to work on, this process will take a while, so take the time and start now.

There is nothing like financial stability and peace of mind. Times can get hard and also be unexpected, so if worse comes to worst and you need money, with the right credit, you could take out a low-interest loan to stay afloat until you figure out a game plan.

Having your credit in good standing is a confidence booster and will help you when you are trying to make decisions that can change your life.

I cannot stress this enough! It will be the smartest thing you can do for yourself. Please, do not wait!

Medical Insurance

So, the first thing we will discuss is medical insurance, especially if you don't have any. If you do have medical insurance, skip this section. But if not, we all know accidents can happen in seconds, and with medical insurance, you will be covered.

Medical insurance can be another not so fun bill to pay, but it is necessary. There are a few available plans you can look into. Some let you choose the deductible; a deductible is a specific amount of money you pay out of pocket before your insurance will pay for services. These can be different amounts but aren't usually too high. It depends on your insurance company, but your policy will also state it.

There are low and no deductible health plans available, but your monthly premium will be higher. There are also high-deductible health plans that have a higher deductible when you go to the doctor, but they will have a lower monthly premium.

Also, some of these plans offer a health savings account option; this savings account is not taxed and can be used for any unexpected out-of-pocket healthcare costs. There is also a tax deduction on these health insurance premiums for self-employed individuals, which will give you added benefits and will reduce the amount you owe in taxes at the end of the year, if any.

You can always look in your area for a local insurance agent to help you find the best insurance to fit your needs and your budget; you can also ask your tax pro to help you with those tax breaks and help you get the most of those savings.

Accidental Insurance

The next is accident insurance. This is a supplemental insurance that is important to have because you never know when accidents or sickness will happen, and your income suddenly stops because you are unable to work.

You can check your local agencies to see what's available in your area. These insurance premiums are often pretty low, depending on the package you decide to pick. But they provide peace of mind in case something unexpected happens and you're unable to work, like a sprained wrist, a twisted ankle, or a car accident. And the benefits are often paid quickly. These insurance policies help with reimbursements of out-of-pocket medical expenses on and off the job and benefits are paid directly to you.

So why not be protected and at least have some money coming back to you when you need it most.

General Liability

So, let's talk about protection insurance in case something unexpected happens while you are working with a client. It is important to consider looking into some sort of liability insurance for your protection. This will protect you if something happens to a client while they are in your place of business. General liability covers the costs of physical injuries and damages, and professional liability protects you if they are harmed from a service you provide or advice you give.

Several insurance companies cover our professional trade; there's even an insurance company for barbers called National Association of Barbers that provide plans such as Insurance Plus that will provide coverage for slip and falls, facial cuts, unsanitary instruments, stolen equipment, chemical/product reactions, and more! They currently have a rate of $169 per year and it covers a number of benefits from professional and general liability, product liability, rental location damage, stolen equipment insurance and more! They also offer part-time barber insurance and student liability insurance as well. This insurance is pretty much a necessity if you pay booth rent in a shop and are considered self-employed. Don't get caught without it!

Retirement

Paying into your retirement is especially important. You want to think about your future when you are young; the earlier you start, the more comfortably you will live later.

The last thing you want to do is turn around and realize you're 40, and think how am I going to live if I have no income or what if something happens ending my career early? Maybe you have health issues, maybe you don't, but your retirement will be here before you know it, and you need time to save for it. Retirement savings must be a priority!

Now is the time to start looking into investment retirement accounts you can start that will enable your money to work for you! There are Solo 401(k), SEP IRA, SIMPLE IRA, Keogh Plan, or Traditional or Roth IRA accounts. Take the time to find a financial advisor or a financial institution that can go over plans and answer any questions you may have before you decide which one fits your needs best. Some companies even offer free or low-cost retirement planning advice to potential clients.

So even if you can't afford much at the beginning, the sooner you start, the more you'll accumulate! The bottom line is to GROW YOUR WEALTH!

Saving Tips

Next, you want to start saving money as soon as you can to set yourself up for success later on in life. We as barbers see a lot of money come and go, and we don't always pay attention to where it goes. You would be surprised by how much you actually waste that could be going toward your future to benefit you.

There are a few important things you should be saving for: taxes, retirement, and emergency savings. These are three things you will definitely thank yourself for later when it comes time to need it. Besides making sure your taxes are paid, creating a financial goal for your future, and being prepared for an emergency are very necessary and key to staying on top of your business.

Saving for important times or long-term financial goals can be difficult, but it can be done, consider this as investing in yourself and taking care of yourself first.

Being a self-employed barber can make it hard to be faithful to saving a specific amount each month because our income fluctuates, but there is a solution for that. Saving a certain amount every month or even every week sounds like a good idea, but let me explain to you why it is not.

First, when you save a certain amount, you are more likely to miss a savings payment to yourself, because maybe it's a slow week and you feel you didn't make enough or if something comes up and you can't afford to contribute. The first thing you will do is make a promise to yourself to put away double next time, but this promise isn't always possible and could throw you off.

Also, the weeks when you are busy and you can afford to put away more, you are still putting away the same amount. You will not be making the most of your savings this way. Therefore, the key is to stick to a certain percentage let's say 25 to 30 percent of your earnings for the week to go toward your three goals. Think of this as paying your future self first!

This way on weeks you make less, you put away less, and the weeks you make more, you will put away more. You are more likely to be consistent with this because you will be basing your savings off your income and your contributions will match your income for that week.

You will be surprised how much you can save with this pay-yourself-first mindset, and the more you save, the more secure you will feel about your future as time goes on.

Another great idea is to look into opening an interest-bearing checking or savings account that will let you make something on the money that you're saving. The only time you will be taking money out of this account is to pay your taxes quarterly, so make sure you are aware of any penalties you may encounter for withdrawals. But no matter what you do, make sure you contribute to your long-term financial goals!

Remember, pay yourself first!

File and Pay Your Taxes

You are a 1099 taxpayer, you want to first establish your business entity, which means getting a business license or creating an LLC and getting your business started as a self-employed individual and then creating your business bank account with your new EIN and begin to collect payments. This is all a part of being a boss and a business owner and so is paying your taxes.

Earlier we talked about saving to pay your taxes. A lot of barbers I know do not file or pay their taxes every year; some not at all.

I know this is a business you could easily just make the cash and pocket it. I also understand it's not an easy world to make it in financially, but this is all the more reason to have a plan and focus on what's best for you and your future.

I know you are saying, especially with everything going on in this world, why is filing and paying taxes so important? Well for example, during 2020 with the Covid-19 crisis, everyone was getting a stimulus check, but a lot of the barbers I knew that never filed and did not pay taxes did not get their stimulus checks. They were waiting and wondering why they never received it, but they were basically unknown to the government and didn't get anything. The people who filed their taxes had their stimulus checks automatically deposited into the bank account that they used to pay or receive their tax refunds. A few barbers I know chose to file after that, and eventually got their stimulus check. But they may have had to make arrangements for the taxes they owed for the last year, if any.

If you have never paid your taxes before, and you have a few years accumulated, don't be afraid, once you do file you may qualify for penalty relief through special IRS waivers such as First Time Abatement, which can remove penalties for filing and paying late if it's your first offense. There are also other penalty relief options based on your circumstances. So, talk to a tax specialist, ask questions, and see what your options are.

Paying your taxes is important because this pays into your self-employment tax for you later on in life. Self-employment tax is basically a tax consisting of Social Security and Medicare primarily for individuals who work for themselves. Generally, your employer would take these taxes out for you and match your contribution, but when you are self-employed, you have to pay the IRS yourself.

However, the self-employment tax will cost you less than you might think because you get to deduct half of your self-employment tax from your net income. Don't worry—find a good tax person, and they will do this all for you! But think of this as a way of paying into your future.

Later, when you're 65 years old, you will have your Social Security benefits to add to your retirement income we talked about earlier. So, if you haven't filed any returns so far and haven't paid your self-employment tax, your earnings for those years won't get counted toward your future Social Security benefits, and this can have a huge impact on your future income and quality of life, so the sooner you start, the better.

Also, while you are entitled to receive your benefits at age 65, if you wait until you're 70, you are eligible for full retirement benefits, so if you chose to wait, your amount will increase. However, each state may be different so check into it if you want to know more about it. Better to be prepared.

This may seem like a long time away for you if you are a young barber, but let me tell you time flies, and the next thing you know, you be looking for all of these things we are discussing, and if you want to be well prepared for your future, start early!

Another important benefit of paying your taxes is being able to prove your income in case you want to buy your first home, car, or any other big item for yourself.

The hardest thing we have as barbers is proving our income, and this is the way we have to do it. Since we don't receive W-2s from an employer, we have to use our tax documents to prove our income. I do believe that recently, mortgage companies will accept bank account statements from the last couple of years as a form of proof, but you would have to check with your realtor.

But hey, don't let all this become overwhelming; there is good news! Filing taxes doesn't mean that you will necessarily owe the IRS. If you are head of household and have dependents you can claim, more than likely you will get money back! And that can be something you can look forward to having as a lump sum when tax time comes around!

Just start saving all your receipts on anything you spend for your business, and be sure to include all the expenses, deductions, and credits you qualify for. The big deductions are health insurance premiums, business insurance (like we discussed earlier), internet and phone, meals, travel, vehicle miles plus gas, repairs etc., booth rent, supplies (tools and products), education (classes, this book! etc.), retirement plan contributions, advertising, tax preparer fees, and so on. These are some of the main ones but there are more!

I know we have been talking about paying taxes, retirement, and saving for emergencies, and maybe this has you worried, but don't let it!

Prioritize these things for yourself and take the time to learn about each of them, one at a time if you have too. You have some time. But, the one thing I have learned, is that in 2020 it has become more apparent that we need to educate ourselves and be more aware of what is actually going on in our life and in the world, so we can prepare for our future and the unexpected.

I know things are hard right now for all of us and things may seem impossible some months, but if you set up your priorities, focus on what you can do, and set the rest as goals, you will do it! Build your clientele, work hard, make a budget for yourself, be aware of where your money is being spent, and plan ahead. You can do this!

If you are new to the barber world and you are still figuring yourself out, that is okay; just make this a goal to strive for and come back to this chapter later if you need to remind yourself.

Start one goal at a time, but ultimately, in the years to come, the goal is to grow as a person, be successful, protect yourself and your family, and live comfortably from a business you not only have your heart invested in but that you have built solely from your passion.

SECTION THREE:

BEYOND THE BARBERSHOP

SECTION THREE:

BEYOND THE BARBERSHOP

"*Decide and Become.*"

Chapter Seven

Starting a New Creative Direction

When you think about expanding your career into a new creative direction, you should be thinking of how to design a career that has the flexibility to grow with you and can get you to financial independence. The goal is to be successful at your own creative vision and live comfortably doing it.

This requires investing in yourself, seeking knowledge, and working toward becoming the best version of yourself. It takes a lot of focus, determination, and consistency to become a freelance barber, start your own product, service, brand, or business, so just be prepared and take it one step at a time.

Earlier in chapter two, we talked about healthy habits and how to find inspiration and maintain your motivation for creativity, so please make sure you refer back to that chapter whenever you need it.

We all need motivation and a creative push from time to time. Sometimes we let time get away from us or throughout the years we become content in the barbershop, and before you know it, we realize that we need and want more. After being in the hair industry for years, it's only natural to want to take your talent, insight, and knowledge to the next level.

There are many paths you can take in the hair industry that can turn into you living out all of your artistic dreams. You are not required to stick with just one vision of being the barber in the barbershop, as a matter of fact as you navigate through this creative industry you have the possibility to create your own vision of success and become as great as you want!

Let's discuss your possibilities!

Be a Mobile or Freelance Barber for Sports, Music, Tv/Film or Agency

There are tons of options to explore in the hair industry, you never know what one client, or one opportunity may bring. Dreaming big, working towards your goals and being consistent with good work ethics can one day lead to your career moving to the next level.

One single decision or opportunity could change your life and put you in places you would have never imagined before. I know a lot of barbers who have chosen to take their talents to different sides of the spectrum, and they love it, so the decision is up to you.

Your vision only has to be clear to you. The decisions you make should depend on the lifestyle you want. Do you like being in one location working regular business hours, making good money where you get to go home every night? or do you want to be an entrepreneur and work at any hour, travel to your clients and enjoy the perks that come from being in that industry?

Being an on-call barber for any of these industries is not easy but can be very rewarding. Let's take a look at a few industries that are in need of mobile and on demand barbers that require 24 hour accessibility for housecalls and travel.

Sports

If your desire is to work with athletes of major sports teams such as football, basketball, soccer, baseball etc., you would most likely be doing housecalls when they are in town or stadium calls before a game. The perks of having these types of clients are possibly traveling to out of town games, cutting them for sports awards, tv shows or interviews, jobs for editorials or commercials and if you are a sports fan, having access to go to the games they are playing; not too bad. The only disadvantage would be if your client got traded to another team, you could be out of a job.

However, the goal of cutting one player would be to offer your services to the rest of the team or to take advantage of the opportunity if some of the players asked for haircuts. The barbers I know that have this type of client account, started from word of mouth, or a player walked into a random barbershop and gave the barber a shot.

It only takes one person to come into the shop and change your life. Your expertise, personality and skill can turn that one engagement into the opportunity you've been waiting for.
All I can say is, be ready!

Music

The music industry is another professional industry that is in high demand for mobile barbers, this includes artists of all genres, that need haircuts, styling, shaves, color, etc. for housecalls, studiocalls, music videos, editorials, tv appearances, award shows, red carpets and more.

Having one artist that is busy can make your schedule demanding and require you to work at a moment's notice and with no days off. Being a part of this industry requires you to dedicate a lot of your time and you must have a creative mindset. You must be very diverse in your cutting skills by being able to create or change hairstyles when your client is looking to change his look.

The best possible advice I can give you, is to get as much experience you can with different textures and styles while you are in the barbershop, to prevent you from being nervous when asked to do something new or having to say you don't know how to do a certain haircut. Like I said before, be ready!

Working with these artists you will have frequent jobs such as music videos, editorials, talk shows, events, award shows and more, so your schedule should be very flexible. The perks of having these types of clients are traveling when needed on tour or for on screen performances and having access to concerts or shows with opportunities to meet and work with other artists as well.

We go more in depth on this in "The Entertainment Industry" chapter later in the book.

Television and Film
In the television and film industry there are a lot of opportunities to work on a continuous basis for movies, talk shows, sitcoms and more, or for Television Networks that have consistent shows with continuous seasons. Some of these projects require you to be a part of the union and some don't, but for more opportunity in movies and film you should be in the union.
Side Note: Another way to work on a movie set without being in the union is if you are brought on by a celebrity you have already been working for.

This side of the industry is great for longevity, and it is usually pretty easy to obtain another job once one show has ended. These jobs tend to have long but structured days and times and are usually paid at a rate that compliments your experience.

Also, because of the amount of time you spend with the talent, you could end up with a permanent client that will request you outside of set as well.

The perks of this industry are the endless creative possibilities and the chance of being recognized for the Make-Up Artists and Hair Stylist Guild Award for an array of categories; this award is given out annually. Plus, the pay and the benefits are not only satisfying, you will get to learn all the secrets and the magic of the movie industry and see your work come to life on the big screen!

Being on sets that are not union allow you to acquire your time and apply it towards your union hours, if that is your end goal. We discuss the Union and its benefits more in depth as well in "The Business Side" chapter later in the book.

Just like in the music industry, if you work for an Actor or Actress off set you will be on call for all the appearances they have, which range from award shows, premieres, talk shows, editorials, readings, parties and more.

The money is good but the convenience of having a barber/groomer come to them for haircuts or beauty services makes for a busy lifestyle. Being a mobile barber is becoming more popular by the day. The demand for people to maintain their desired look is wanted at all costs, and they will expect for you to make the sacrafices and arrangements to be there when needed.

Agency
Along with being a personal barber to the elite, some prefer to aim their efforts towards working for a reputable top agent who represents Hair and Make-up Artists doing Photoshoots, Editorials, Commercials, Advertising, Fashion Campaigns with celebrities for major magazines and brands.

If you are a Barber, you may want to consider being a male groomer which is where you would do light makeup for the client as well. I find it's rare to have a barber that does light makeup in the entertainment business in any aspect; they usually have to hire two people, but if you can manage to do both, it will not only get you hired first, it will make you more money, set you apart from the rest and even better make you more valuable.

If you are desiring to join this side of the industry, depending on your experience, you may have to be an assistant to a hairstylist or groomer to learn the ropes before you go on your own.

Having an agent represent you will not only pave the way for you to gain other opportunities you wouldn't otherwise have access too, but they will also handle your negotiations for top pay, create your invoices for all your jobs, and make sure you have a deal memo in place prior to your job for all required terms and conditions.

Having this representation has many perks such as high paying gigs with A-list celebrities for top magazines and brands, the opportunity to work with top photographers, travel, and the chance for you to continue to work with these celebrities on an ongoing basis.

The opportunities are endless, and the experiences are priceless. We discuss having an agent more in depth later in chapter 10 "The Business Side".

All of these careers are amazing and have great perks so and if being a mobile or freelance barber for any of these industries is something that you want to focus on, here are a few tips to follow!

* Take every opportunity you have to enhance your knowledge, skills, techniques and versatility with different looks and styles.

* Make sure you are confident and willing to adjust to any situation and keep a strong mindset.

* Start now to build a portfolio of your best work and be ready to send it when requested.

*Market your services by offering to do housecalls to clients who are willing to pay for
the accessibility and your talent; even if they are your regular clients! This will give you the opportunity to get used to house calls and what it takes to be prepared.

When you work in different environments outside the shop it will help prevent any problems or mistakes, later when it counts!

Remember, we have a special talent which means you can create a special career out of it. Don't forget timing is everything, so trust the process! Prepare yourself along the way and you will be fine when your opportunity comes along. Be fearless when pursuing any of these amazing industries; do not underestimate your superpower!

Starting a Business
When you are looking to expand your creative vision, there are a lot of directions you can go in this industry and the possibilities are endless. But

regardless of the direction you take, you will need to go through a series of steps so that you can have an idea of where to start.

I hope these steps can help you get started on creating a path to turn your Topbarber idea into a reality. I created a section in the back of this book for you to take notes, put ideas down and write out your goals, so highlight the important steps, take your time, do more research, and breathe.

This will no doubt be a lot of work, but ultimately, it will be an extension of your creative dream and your contribution to yourself and this incredible industry you are a part of. You have already invested in yourself when you decided to go to school with your vision to become a barber, so this too will be an investment, but it will be so worth it; YOU are worth it!

Let's get right into it. Here is an example.

Let's say you want to express yourself and create your own quality hair product you can be proud of, not only to use on your own clients but also to share with the world.

This is a general idea of creating a product to get you started. But having an idea of something that interests you or will solve a problem for consumers will be the first step in creating that great product. You will want to do some research on similar products for ingredients, pricing, bottle type, and labeling, then decide what you like about it or what you want to change. Write down any ideas or information you have found.

Next, start the process of creating your product, and once you love it, you will want to do a product run of samples and begin to set your product up for marketing. All of this will take time but it's okay to take your time, enjoy the process, and get it right.

Once you have spent some time on the creation and perfecting your product you will want to run a substantial product run to get feedback from your customers. This will take time but while that's in progress you can create your business plan in steps, it will include your financial strategy (for samples, packaging, creating the product, etc.), business structure along with any insurance, etc., finding a chemist of your choice, length of time to produce your product and to create samples, and last but very importantly, finishing your test run. Also, allow time for creative mistakes — we all make them.

Here are the steps we talked about above in detail, and hopefully this will help give you an idea and insight on starting your next adventure!

Step 1: Come up with an idea and get a feel for what you want to invest yourself in. Be prepared to do your research and find what you love. Keep your eyes and ears open to ideas and new feelings, because when you are excited and you keep the passion, it will help you drive this idea into fruition faster. You have to see it in your mind, feel it in your heart and know it in your soul. This goes for any time throughout your life when you want to create change. This will ensure that throughout the process of bringing your idea to life and after the success of it you will never feel like you're working.

Step 2: Create a plan. This plan is almost like making a blueprint of your ideas. You have to visualize your end goal and make a step-by-step written out plan for how you will get there. So, start doing the research and gather all the information you need about your creation. Also, it's a good idea to predict what some of the hurdles might be and write out how you will get over them. For instance, in the example above you will research all ingredients, pricing, and you will need to find and decide on bottle types and labeling. Figure out what will economically and effectively work for you. Don't forget to write down what you like, any idea changes and information you have found.

Step 3: Plan your finances and get them in order. Go through your plan and write down what all the expenses will be. Be as specific as possible. Do your research to plan for additional expenses that could come up. Look at the costs for licensing permits and insurance. Ask someone who has done something similar if you are forgetting anything. Your financial strategy is important to have in detail from the very beginning in order for your business to be lucrative and successful.

At this point you can start creating your product or idea and preparing it for perfection. This will be a trial and error phase but that is to be expected, be patient do not rush this process. In the meantime, you can move on to step 4.

Step 4: When it's time to start your new business, choose a business structure, are you going to be a sole proprietor (independent), a partnership (you have a partner), an LLC, or a corporation? Different entities offer different benefits to your business. You can do a lot of research online for yourself to get an idea of terminology and questions to ask, but talk to a tax person, business attorney, or business advisor to choose the business structure that will fit your business the best.

Step 5: Once you decide on a business structure, pick, and register your business name. Do we even need to discuss how important this is? Choosing your new name is vital to your successful business. Think about this intensely. Write some ideas down, have at least two options in case one is taken, ask some trusted friends their opinion, embrace the name, and own it before you choose it. You really need to consider and make sure you are totally happy and satisfied with it because changing it will be a difficult process. Let the name represent you and the direction of your new creative journey. Once you are completely happy with it, go register it and make it official!

Step 6: Get licenses and permits. We touched on this in step three. Depending on what type of business or brand you are planning on starting, you will have to obtain a few required licenses and permits. If you find a professional to help you setup your business structure, they should also be familiar with any permits or licenses you will need, or you can look up under your city and state and see what is required for your type of business.

Step 7: Get your team together and ready. They will help you with social media, marketing, content curation and anything you need so you can focus on creating the product. This may require time and energy trying to find people that believe in your vision that are very supportive and are just as motivated as you are. These people should be consistent, have a great work ethic, great ideas, goal oriented and add value to your business. They should be a genuine asset.

Step 8: Finalize all of your ideas and moves you have made so far. Make sure you have crossed all your t's and dotted all your i's. These steps should pretty much complete your process and you should feel good where you are at this point.

So, get ready to start promoting your business and watch it evolve!

Step 9: Promote your creation and begin marketing. There are several ways to market your product or business. You can make appearances and go to local marketing events and spread the word by introducing yourself and passing out your business cards and/or samples.

These in-person techniques are always good because they give people a sense of your personality and your able to give your authentic energy and vision to make your product relatable to the consumer. However, another way to achieve this is by social media marketing and content marketing. They are the most popular and the most up to date current strategies because of the explosive internet craze.

In these next few paragraphs, we will discuss marketing with social media, content creating and branding.

Marketing

The internet makes it easier for you to get your product or newly established business out there into the view of millions of people without even leaving your home. The internet is the most powerful tool we have these days and is essential to any business. All you need is a camera, a video camera, internet access and a creative mind. Basically, with all of our technology like social media apps, and our phones you have what you need at your fingertips to get started.

Social Media Marketing Strategies

Marketing with social media has never been easier. If you are not computer or social media savvy, devoting your time to doing a lot of research and taking a few marketing, computer, and business classes would help you on your journey to becoming a successful entrepreneur. No one can take away your education, so why not empower yourself?

There are reported to be one billion active people on Instagram every month! People tend to check their Instagram accounts on average between 24 and 32 times a day. And more than 25 billion businesses use Instagram to capture attention, spark interest, create desire, and gain customers. Over 130 million users engage with shopping posts every month. And all these people using Instagram are potential customers to your product or brand.

So, creating a marketing strategy based on Instagram alone might be one of the best ways to not only gain new customers and spread the word about your product or service but will also cost you nothing but your time and effort. This makes marketing your product easy from the comfort of your own home or on the go.

Aside from using Instagram there are other social media platforms for marketing your new product, brand, or service, so here are some strategies along with popular social media outlets to help you create your online presence that is only a few clicks away.

You should not only plan on exploring Instagram, which is linked to Facebook, but also Snapchat, YouTube videos, and the most popular in my opinion Tik Tok. Tik Tok's algorithm is easier to work with to build a following, they also have Tik Tok shop that makes it easy to sell products. All these outlets mostly go hand in hand which connects them from one to the other. With the popularity of these social sites, you can take your product to the next level in no time.

Social media allows you to present your product or company to the world with a strategic plan and focus on main points and unique characteristics of any aspect of your business that you want your customers to focus on. This will also help you create a brand for your company. People should be able to find you on every platform. Because social media is diversifying, think about which social media platform, if not all, will be the most beneficial to your company or brand and start there first.

The internet is crucial to the success of your company, product, idea, or brand. As a new or existing business owner, you will have a lot of other responsibilities that need your attention, and you will be working on multiple tasks a day. This is why we talked earlier about developing a team to help you stay consistent, so you are not overwhelmed, start procrastinating or slowly fall behind. Focusing on more than one major task can lead to nothing getting effectively done. Keeping up with promoting your business on all your social media outlets can become a great deal of work.

You definitely need to be hands on and aware of what your business needs to ensure success, and you also want to oversee any decision that needs to be made, so when these tasks begin to be too much, don't get overwhelmed, give some of these duties to the person on the team you structured.

Content Marketing

Let's dive a little deeper with your content and how important it is to be consistent, because even if you enjoy content marketing, you will probably be too busy to do it all. Content on every one of your social media platforms is important because it builds a relationship and trust with your audience and stimulates their interest in your product or company. It brings awareness and excitement as you are building. This can be anything from creating posts, videos, Vlogs, or Spotify lists.

My tip is to look into content marketing strategies and online tools to help you as well as split small jobs up between one or two other people on your team. Whether you are running a business or just creating a product, you will have a lot of ground to cover, so if you can discuss some strategies with someone, bounce ideas off each other or use online tools to help do the work for you, do it!

This way your obligations don't feel as heavy, you will free up space in your mind and it helps you put your focus on other things that need your attention.

Branding

Branding is different than creating a company, it makes a statement that represents your company, like a recognizable logo, symbol, or name. Let's take Nike for example, when you see the swoosh, you know it is Nike. Creating a brand is a global term and has everything to do with strong marketing. As you market your business, the key is to do it with specific branding in mind from the very beginning. What type of characteristics or voice do you want your company to have? Your brand's voice should be similar to a personality. You want it to feel relatable. Ask yourself, what does your company sound like? What does it value? What problems does it solve? Your company needs to have its own voice and sound, and the goal is to be recognizable to your customers or potential customers on social media. You want people to expect this sound or voice from your company, and you want this sound or voice to be associated with your brand every time. So put your creative cap on and start brainstorming — what will it be?

Remember, every piece of content you create whether its text, image, or video should match your branding goals.

This is important to think about from the start, so you have an idea where to direct your product or company's attention. You want your company to stand for something and speak volumes without even saying anything. You want it to be recognizable and trusted just by seeing the logo. This takes dedication, powerful marketing, and most of all, consistency and time.

Your brand will ultimately represent you, so what do you stand for?

I know this is a lot of information, especially if you are just dipping into the idea of starting your brand or business, or barely stepping into the hair industry for that matter, but it gives you something to think about, and I say why not have the information there when you need it or are ready and have a head start.

You are an amazing, creative entrepreneur to have entered this industry in the first place, so don't be nervous to move forward and take things to the next level. Take it one step at a time, start small, don't rush into it, think it through, and enjoy the entire journey from beginning to end, because this idea, product, service, company, or brand will be a reflection of you and all your hard work.

Trust me, when the time comes, your passion will drive you and your anticipation for success will take control. It's not about when you start its about where you finish. This will be a remarkable and exciting journey for you, and you will be so proud to watch your career evolve. Like this book is for me, in so many ways it will be the most rewarding thing you have ever created!

"...being a creative is powerful and we thrive through constant inspiration."

Chapter Eight

Hair Shows

My confidence and talent throughout my career were always in the want and need of growth. I was always eager to learn anything I could that had to do with hair, so when hair shows came to my area, I was there. I started going to hair shows because of my love for cutting hair and I was obsessed with this industry. I encourage you to go as well; these shows are very inspirational, always an experience and have the newest tools for sale from some of the biggest clipper and beauty companies, plus an array of different types of educational classes to take.

When I first started cutting hair, I realized that being a creative is powerful and we thrive through constant inspiration. I was always saving my money and taking the time out of my schedule to enjoy all three days of walking around, watching demos, taking classes and buying all the newest tools. I have taken the same clipper classes year after year, just incase I missed something from the year before, I was truly inspired. This became a tradition for me, even if I went alone. Hair shows were special to me, and it wasn't long before I realized I wanted to be a part of it no matter how long it took.

Hair shows, also known as beauty trade shows, are typically spread out over a few days and bring together barbers and hairstylists from all over. They are filled with new products, top influencers in the industry, tons of sneak peeks, educational classes, some celebrity appearances, and connections you couldn't get anywhere else!

On the West Coast in Southern California, we have one major show called International Salon and Spa Expo (ISSE), also frequently called The Long Beach Expo. This is the largest cash-and carry professional beauty event on the West Coast that provides endless inspiration to boost the attendees' careers and creativity. The show celebrated its 20th anniversary in January 2019, so it is one of the longest running hair shows around.

During my years of doing this show, 2007–2013, it mainly focused on hair, skincare, and beauty; it was fun, but it was mostly for hairstylists. Only a small portion was dedicated to barbering which came from two of the biggest clipper companies, Andis and Wahl. Similar shows are The Beauty Experience in Las Vegas, International Beauty Show in NYC, America's Beauty Show in Chicago, and Premiere in Orlando, Florida.

These larger shows usually have tons of classes available from almost every distributor; some are paid, and some are free. Classes consist of haircutting, styling, product knowledge, and hands-on workshops. Andis, Wahl, Babyliss, and other clipper brands hold quite a few classes, teaching about their diffcrent tools, techniques and answering questions at select times throughout the day.

There are also large booths with stage shows going on simultaneously throughout the venue. These shows tend to be exciting with tons of people, music blaring, and an endless number of products and tools for sale.

There are only a few barber shows that are available to attend, and they are, Barbercon which was launched in 2016, and gets bigger every year and shows in different cities throughout the US, CT Barber Expo in Hartford, CT, and Behind the Chair in San Antonio, Texas. These shows not only have the top clipper companies and barber brands to see, but it's also a great opportunity to take classes, watch platform artists perform the latest haircuts, network within the barber community, and attend or enter a barber battle.

On a smaller scale, you have hair shows that are held in hotel ballrooms in different cities. The space is very limited, but they do have quite a few companies that hold demos of haircutting and styling. Although they sell pretty much everything for hair, they don't bring out tons of products or tools because space and sales are limited.

These shows are mainly distributors and local companies that will only bring out their highest selling products and tools. These smaller shows usually hold barber battles and hair competitions.

Back in the day, these battles would draw a lot of barbers from all over, either attending to watch or entering to win. I had the opportunity for a few years to be a judge from Andis and hand out awards to the winners, that was a proud moment for me.

I was always excited to do this; I saw a lot of talented barbers from all over come out and be amazing. It was fun and inspiring to witness all the talent and to be a judge for a company I loved and for a career I had so much passion for. I have to say, I was honored to do it! The shows I did were once a year in Los Angeles and in Northern California. All these shows, including the larger ones, were in about five different cities up and down the West Coast as well as in Las Vegas and Arizona. To this day, the show in Long Beach and Vegas hold the reign for being the largest hair shows on the West Coast. I always loved going to any of the shows and soaking up as much knowledge as I could.

Before I started going to these hair shows I was already infatuated with Andis and wanted to work for them. I had sent in a couple of portfolios and was just waiting to be accepted. I figured it may take a while. In the meantime, I went to the same show every year to get as much education as I could. I would frequent the same booths to see what new tools were out and began to know some of the distributors from different companies as well.

 One distributor I met had a huge beauty supply business, they had clippers, hairdryers, curling irons, flatirons, and styling tools. After seeing me there often and talking to me every year, he asked me if I would like to get on the platform and demo the tools to show people how to use them and answer any questions they may have. Although my love was just for barbering and my passion was to work with Andis Clipper Company, I was not going to turn down any opportunities. I was nervous at first, but I loved it!

After that first day, I offered my services to him whenever he needed a stylist. I eventually began to do all the shows with him from Long Beach to the smaller shows in Los Angeles all the way to Las Vegas. I learned a lot from him and gained a lot of confidence and experience on stage interacting and talking to people. I worked for him for about four years in total. It was a lot of work, but we had a lot of fun.

Being at all the shows allowed me to meet and talk to a lot of people from a lot of different companies. But at the time working for Andis was my dream job, and I would always make my way over there to watch their platform artists do haircuts and answer questions, and before the show ended for the day, I would purchase each and every new tool they released.

Sometime later, I was approached about working for Wahl, which is a huge clipper company and longtime competitor of Andis. They were looking for a platform artist, and I was recommended. They told me if I was interested to give their office a call. Although I am a fan of their tools, I thought about it and hesitated because at the time I really wanted to work for Andis. I wanted to wait for them because I believed in these tools like I believed in myself. It was all I had ever used since the beginning of my career. And to be honest, I knew everything about Andis' tools and nothing about Wahl.

After much consideration, I did reach out to them, and I turned in an application and my portfolio. To my surprise, Lance Wahl, the company's global vice president of professional products, reached out to me and offered me a position as a platform artist.

I knew that if I took this job my chances of working with Andis would be slim to none. Like I said, they are huge competitors in the clipper industry, dating back to the beginning of both companies. However, I accepted the invitation, and I was set up to watch a class that another female barber was instructing so I could see how it was supposed to go.

Although my passion was to work as a platform artist at these hair shows, my bigger passion was to work for the company of my choice. This day made me realize that I was there for the wrong reasons. I didn't feel as though I was following what I believed in, so at the end of the day, I turned the job down in hopes of one day working for Andis.

Two years later, with more inquires and two more job applications with portfolios, I finally got the chance to come to a show and fill in for a weekend with Andis! I was so excited and proud to be there! But I was really nervous.

It was definitely a challenge because the stage was a lot bigger than what I was used to, and many barbers were coming to the booth to watch and ask questions, so I couldn't act as if this was my first time up there. I had to do a great job on every haircut plus answer questions correctly because all eyes were on me, and there was no time for mistakes. This first day was very intimidating and super exhausting, but I was so grateful, and I couldn't believe I finally had the opportunity to work for a company that I had waited so long to work for. My first day was long and tiring, and the weekend was even longer.

It was so much busier and more intense than what I was used to. It was nonstop, but I have to say that the two years leading up to this moment, working on stage, really helped prepare me for all of it. It was almost the same —just on a larger scale. At the time of my hiring, I was still working for my distributor, and my schedule became too hectic to do both. He understood and was happy for me. It was time for me to move on.

When I officially got hired for Andis, they flew me to Wisconsin to train, sign paperwork, and to see the headquarters. I had to learn about all their tools (which I was pretty familiar with already) and how to properly present them on stage and how to sell them. I worked three-day weekends in Long Beach, Los Angeles, Seattle, Las Vegas, and Arizona. It was always fun and challenging but hard work as well.

When I did platform work, I had to find models to cut and demonstrate different tools in our line and be able to inspire and educate people that stood around the stage. I had to keep their attention and try to get them to expand their tool collection.

Aside from stage presence, finding a model to demonstrate on was always the hardest part. The type of model I was looking for depended on what tool I was using and what type of haircut I would be doing. People were already showing up to hair shows looking their best, so this was often a task, but it always worked out.

When I was doing the haircuts in front of the crowd, I had to explain every step and answer any questions they had about my technique or the tool I was using. I had to be savvy with my words, and even though I had my favorite tools I loved to use, I had to be familiar with every tool we had in the line and know them all like the back of my hand.

This is why it is so important to know different styles and how to cut all textures and types of hair because to do these hair shows, you really have to be versatile and be able to flex your skills and talent confidently. Even though I felt confident in my cutting skills, I was still a little intimidated and nervous because I was in front of a bunch of creative individuals who were looking for all the answers and perfect haircuts every time.

If this is one of your goals, you will have a lot of fun and become very experienced. Along with platform work, you will also be doing floor work. This involves talking to customers who are barbers, stylists, and students, answering all their questions about all tools and products.

Over a three-day weekend, you will sell tons of tools and products, and on the last day, you will help clean up and pack up anything that didn't sell. It can be exhausting because you will be standing on your feet, talking, and running around for about a 10- to 12-hour day, but you will be able to add every tool the company makes to your arsenal, travel, and meet a lot of great creative people like yourself. Even though all of this makes for hard work and an extremely long weekend, it is also very rewarding.

Nowadays, along with your commitment to the hair shows and doing classes when you can, these companies will expect for you to promote and post on social media as often as possible. So, in the meantime, work on your versatility, cutting skills and your social media presence.

Being a barber influencer takes time, and some getting used to, especially if you are not an extroverted person. Plus, make sure you keep your business and personal posts professional. This will work towards your advantage if you want to be a part of your favorite clipper company's team.

❝ *It's nobody else's fault if you don't fulfill any of your goals or passions. No matter how unreachable they may seem.* ❞

Chapter Nine
The Entertainment Industry

This is a chapter that is very, very special to me. Being involved in the entertainment industry has been the biggest, most life-changing experience of my entire life. It has changed and enhanced my life in so many ways; it is really unbelievable. I love what I do and who I do it for and wouldn't change it for the world. It gets tough at times with a lot of ups and downs and many valuable learning experiences, some harder than others for sure. It has literally tested my faith, integrity, and the confidence that I had in myself, but through it all, it has made me so much stronger, smarter, and confident than I have ever been or could have imagined being.

To be in this industry, you have to be driven, hardworking, resilient, and very dependable. You will be making sacrifices in almost every aspect of your life. It is a lifestyle that is unpredictable with very little sleep and little to no vacations. However, it is also the most amazing, exciting, rewarding, gratifying, and enriching job ever!

Surrounding Yourself With The Right People

There are a lot of things to expect from this industry. Life can and will be hectic, and it's important to remember that your time is the most valuable asset you have. You will be spreading your time between work, family, and if you're lucky, a social life with your friends. You will go through a lot with the people you love; some will be in your corner rooting for you, but to your surprise, some will also be unsupportive. With limited free time, you will realize that you will need to be picky and choosy about who you spend your time with and give your energy to.

For myself, I don't have much time to spend with too many people outside of my family, but I do enjoy being around like-minded people who carry the same type of work ethic and who are striving for great achievements. They don't necessarily have to be in the same industry but knowing you're not the only one with a hectic schedule and other goals you are trying to accomplish, makes it more tolerable and seems not that impossible.

It's quite the creative push to see or hear of someone that is just as busy and determined as you are in accomplishing their goals, it helps you stay on track to accomplishing yours. Inspiring each other is what we are here for regardless of our end goal.

These types of people always tend to exchange good empowering energy that help me turn my stress into motivation. In this industry, your job will become your priority, and even though you will spend a lot of time alone, this doesn't mean you have to feel alone in your own journey.

This is when you learn the most about yourself and you are able to get your thoughts in order. Whenever you get the opportunity to be around some of the talented people you work with or someone who is on a similar mission, take advantage of it to help fuel your own productivity.

You will have a lot of responsibility coming from all directions, and despite the challenges you will also have an opportunity to be just as great as the people you surround yourself with.

How I Got Started in the Music Business

People always ask me how I made it into this industry, so I think that sharing some of my experiences will help you understand what this industry entails and how much dedication it takes to work in it.

I started with one goal, achieved it, and went to the next. With each goal, I was driven by passion. I had no fear of attaining what I wanted and no doubt I could do it; I just knew it would be a matter of time.

Although I have achieved most of my aspirations, I still feel there are other accomplishments I want to achieve. Having the desire to achieve greatness in your life, no matter what part of life you are in is important because we should always strive to grow as a person and be the best version of ourselves we can be. Alot of times personal issues, the wrong people or distractions can get in the way of our focus and distract us from our goals. It makes the process take longer. There can be so much going on in our lives that can prevent us from what we want or distract us from our goals. The key is to have tunnel vision and let all those distractions go. Think and know what you want, prepare for it, keep going and when the timing is right you will have it.

Do not limit yourself in this limitless world.

From the Barbershop.

While working at the barbershop, doing stage work at hair shows, I had just started to work for Andis Clipper Company for about a year or so and I was thinking about pursuing the entertainment industry to work for music artists; to cut them and their entire teams. I felt like I had enough experience, and I was ready for the change in my career. This was a rapidly growing industry, especially within rap, and I knew I would be able to evolve in it and start a whole new level of business for myself. This dream and goal became more and more vivid in my mind every day. The more I thought about it, the more I wanted and knew I could do it.

I lived and worked in a barbershop about 60 miles east of Hollywood and had no idea how I was going to accomplish this idea. Not to mention, I was very focused on doing hair shows as often as possible and in between I was also doing private classes for Andis at barbershops and hair schools throughout Southern California. I was also taking business classes at a community college part-time near my house, as well as being part-time at the barbershop. I was very busy, but I loved it.

During my promotion for my cutting classes, I met a guy who was a promoter for a nightclub, and he also managed a barbershop in the MidWilshire area in LA. We had a meeting about doing a class at his barbershop, and during the conversation, he offered me a booth at his shop and told me he would do commission if I was interested. I thought about it for a couple of weeks because it was definitely going to be a sacrifice for me to travel out there with no guarantee that I was going to make any money in a new environment with no clientele. Not to mention, I had a truck that wasn't very dependable. But I knew I wanted to get into the entertainment industry and work for music artists.

I figured they would need the convenience of a mobile barber for videos, interviews, and performances they had. To do this, I knew I would have to put myself near the area I wanted to work in. So, after I weighed the pros and cons, I took him up on his offer to work part time at his barbershop.

When I shared my plans with the owner of the shop where I worked, who was also a friend, she told me that working in the entertainment business isn't all that it is cracked up to be, and I was wasting my time. She also said if I was going to do that, I needed to come off of part-time and start paying full booth rent for the week. I was surprised and a little thrown off: I would still be there on the same days and hours. She said it was because I would be making more money. I said, "I don't even have any clients out there yet," Shortly after, the conversation was over. I said to myself I'll just worry about that later and walked away. I knew I didn't have all the answers and I was taking a risk, but I also knew what I wanted, and I was willing to make the sacrifice. I wasn't going to let anything stop me.

I absolutely know now that if I had let that discourage me, I would not be where I am today, and more than likely, I probably wouldn't have written this book. So, I will take all the credit for that!

I share this story because I'm proof that you shouldn't let anybody stop you from going after your dreams. It's nobody else's fault if you don't fulfil any of your goals or passions no matter how unreachable they seem.

You have to take all the responsibility for not only all of your successes but your failures as well, and although some are hard to take, failures are going to teach you resilience and allow you to grow in the most unique ways. You don't want to regret later in life not pursuing something because of fear or lack of support.

Just make sure you are making safe decisions with good intentions that will help you grow as a person. Being the best version of yourself is always the goal.

To the Industry

It didn't take long for me to start gaining new clients, and six months later I ended up catapulting myself right into my aspiration of being in the entertainment industry. Although I was new to it, I was always ready to work and before I knew it business took off and I have been on the move ever since. I was on call, running from set to set, studios and house calls for several major artists. Being on-call and traveling to private locations became essential.

Grooming became more in demand and having someone available who they could trust to meet their grooming needs, no matter where they were, even if it was just a haircut, was becoming more and more necessary. It quickly became a requirement for me to be available 24 hours a day, seven days a week, so keep this in mind if you want to be in this industry.

My life continues to revolve around theirs to where I have to take my dinner to go sometimes just to meet their needs promptly or wake up out of my sleep at 2 a.m. to do a last-minute house call. Taking time to myself is nonexistent and vacations, if I can manage to take one, needs to be planned around their upcoming schedule.

This is a phenomenal job that allows you to be surrounded by amazing people, incredible energy, and mind-blowing situations. Just know, you will sacrifice a lot for it.

Sean is my Kanye

Although I only worked at the shop in LA three days a week, one night my co-workers and I were at the shop late to clean up after watching the Lakers' game. Around midnight a guy came in with his friend and said, "Can I get a haircut?" No one was willing to do it since we were closed, but I said, "Sure I'll do it!" Once I started cutting his hair, we started having a conversation. He told me he just moved out here and he raps, and I shared that I wanted to work on sets and cut artists' hair, so if he ever needed anyone, I could do it. I finished him up and gave him my number. A couple of days later, he called me close to midnight (again) as I was heading home and said, "Are you going to be in that shop you were at tomorrow morning? I have an interview I'm doin' and just want to get cleaned up."

I said, "No, I'm only in there a couple of days a week, but where are you now?"

He told me, and I happened to be a couple of blocks away. He sent me the address, so I turned the car around and went over. That night was the beginning of my career in this amazing industry. My career grew alongside his, and his incredible work ethic was an inspiration to me to keep working towards my dream.

I believe it was meant for me to be in the shop that night, and he was meant to come into my life and make everything that I had been wanting for to happen. This is exactly what happens when you manifest something that you believe in with no doubt and no fear. Two weeks after meeting him my LA shop I worked at closed down, and my career in the entertainment industry began.

Ironically, about four years later, he taught me about manifesting and I realized that is exactly what I was doing by following my dreams with no doubt and no fear and it is ultimately how we met. It always amazes me when I think of that day and where I was in my life. I am forever grateful for that moment. We were both new in this industry and we both worked extremely hard to get where we are today.

I watched him build his entire career himself. He worked sick or not, and therefore, so did I. We did what we had to do for our passion with no questions asked. I was there every time he needed me no matter what. He inspired me tremendously, and we had so much in common because, although we had a different path, our dreams matched.

Throughout the time we worked together, he introduced me to everyone he knew as his barber and told them if they ever needed one to let him know. Although I built a lot of my own relationships along the way, he was always very supportive and opened many doors for me. He gave me my start by believing in me, and I will always appreciate and love him for that. He will always, no matter what, be family to me. We went on to do tons of music videos, TV shows, red carpet events, commercials, and editorials for some of the biggest magazines, concerts, and more!

The Most Important Rules

Once I became immersed in this industry, I had to understand it came with a lot of responsibilities, not only with my time, but with some mandatory standards. With this highly demanding job, you must understand the rules that come with it. You have to learn how to keep things in perspective and understand how to handle situations in order to maintain your credibility.

Being a celebrity barber is not an easy profession. I understand it looks fun from the outside, and don't get me wrong, it is an extraordinary job, but it is also a job that requires a ton of commitment and the mindset to be prepared for anything. There are a lot of rules that are set in place and traits you should carry in order to maintain your job.

Four of the biggest traits to develop and rules to understand in this industry are loyalty, the ability to separate your personal life and work life, the ability to not take things personally, and good work ethics. Let's talk about them.

Loyalty

Not only does this job take sacrifice, but it also takes loyalty. An artist trusting you is one of the biggest compliments. They need to trust not only that you will make them look good, which is a major part of it, but also that they can allow you to be around their personal life. You will be in their home, around their friends and family, and may hear private conversations and music that hasn't been released yet, so loyalty and trust are essential in your relationships with them. Respecting their privacy and space is of utmost importance in this business and knowing when to leave the room and give them privacy without being told is also important to be aware of.

If you want to keep your job, remember privacy is rule number one! You may have to sign an NDA (Non-Disclosure Agreement) before you start working with your client whether you are in his home, recording studio or on set; this is an agreement you sign to not discuss, photograph, or repeat anything you see or hear, but whether your client has an NDA or not, you should treat all of your clients with the same respect to their privacy.

Never invite any friends or even family with you until you are absolutely positive it is okay to do so, and you may even want to give them a heads up and ask before just to see what kind of response you get. You never know what is going on or who may be over there. Don't forget this is your job, and they are your boss.

Do not take pictures without permission or post any content that is being filmed, most of the time you are not allowed to video or take pictures while on set, but if you do happen to take some, you shouldn't post them until it is okay to do so. I rarely post pictures of my clients unless it's of my work, and I always wait until he posts them first.

Do not overstay your visit, after you are done with your service, clean up, make sure they don't need anything else and leave. Again, learn how to read the room and know when to walk out to give privacy. Also, don't invite yourself to events.

Do not give addresses out, ever! Giving out their address without permission violates not only their privacy but their health and safety. For example, resist the temptation to tell a rideshare driver who you are headed to see; I have been in some where the driver will spark up a conversation to figure out what you do and what you are headed to do. At all costs keep your client your priority; their privacy and safety are paramount.

There are a lot of rules and regulations in this industry to commit to, but they are mostly common sense; it's always best to first consider what is in the best interest of your client.

Another word of advice—never tell your clients' business to another artist you work with or to anyone else for that matter. Be mindful of your conversations, if you start telling them someone else's business, they may think you are telling theirs as well. As a matter of fact, if you can help it, keep the business that you do with other artists to yourself. You may think it's reputable and cool to tell an artist that you work with, that you also work with a lot of other artists or where you might be going next, but in reality, especially if you are just starting to work with someone, I suggest you keep what you do and who you do it for to yourself. Some of them just like the fact that you are there for them and are not interested in who else you are around. Plus, believe it or not, not all artists get along, and they might feel like you could go and tell their business, because they don't know you that well yet. It could cost you your job.

It is better in any situation to stay neutral in these matters and just be there to give a great service, build your credibility, and do your job.

Another big issue is to never talk about the music any of them are working on to other people; they most likely don't want what they are working on or have coming out to be discussed with other people. That is theirs to share.

Separate Your Personal Life and Work Life

The first thing I learned in this industry was to keep your personal life and your business life separated. Once I learned that it wasn't a good idea to mix them, I began to keep them totally separate. I quickly found out that it's just easier to keep them apart, otherwise it will put you in situations you would rather not want to be in, so I can keep my business and the business of my clients private. It's understandable that some people like to ask questions but it's important for you to respect your privacy and the privacy of your client.

In the beginning, it's a given you will want to share all of the exciting moments you are involved in. As this becomes your everyday life, problems or situations will happen that you will want to discuss with someone close to you, this is hard, but I suggest you don't.

This is where the part of respecting your clients' confidentiality comes into play, and since these work issues are not average problems, they will always be new and intriguing to who you're telling. Additionally, there is no benefit in telling them as they will never see your problem or have a solution because they don't understand a life they aren't a part of or can't imagine, and they are maybe too focused on who it is about than to understand there's even a problem.

It can be hard to share things about the entertainment industry with people outside of it because they are often unable to look at things from a practical point of view. This can make you feel like no one understands, and you can often feel alone. But because of all the people you work around and the work ethic you develop, you will come to realize that this just comes with the industry you are in, and you have to respect it.

One example, when you receive a call for a haircut in the middle of the night and you're asleep, you have to get up and go. This is very common by the way. In this industry, we all work hard and at all times of the day or night, and we do what we have to do to make sure things get done.

Often, someone would ask me why I was so tired, and I'd say, "I had to work in LA last night, I got home at five this morning", and they would say "You're crazy. I wouldn't be going to LA, staying out all night, hope it was worth it." And me being very tired but knowing I had too because it is my jobs responsibility, it is unconceivable for most.

It just seems like very few people actually understand the work ethic that is involved. And yes, it is worth it, but it's also your job, and it just shows that this job isn't for everybody.

Unfortunately, entitlement or the misunderstanding of you not being able to include certain people into your work life, can cause hurt feelings, so be prepared to lose some people in the process, this is normal; it's hard for people to adjust to a life you are choosing to live that can't always involve them.

It can get difficult at times, but everyone in this industry has sadly experienced this at one point or another, but just stay focused, keep moving forward, and try not to take it too personally. It will all work out.

You will also be involved in a lot of private moments with your clients that are not yours to share. As this becomes part of your life, people are always going to be curious and want to know what is going on. At times they will ask questions, but remember, this is your job, and like we discussed earlier, your clients' privacy is a priority, so keep it short and as simple as possible.

Sometimes people will choose to go and discuss you and your work life with others, and you just don't know what they are going to say. For me, it became easier to just not discuss it or I downplay any situations I'm in for the sake of my privacy, not just my clients'. In a lot of ways, having my privacy always made things easier for me. I learned the less people know the better. Once in this industry, you never know who genuinely wants to be your friend for you or who wants to be your friend to hopefully be around the people you know.

Don't Take Anything Personal!

Taking things personally can be discouraging whether its professionally or in your personal life. In this industry you have to learn to disregard a lot of things, or your feelings will be hurt. It's about building your mindset and It's important to realize that everything cannot be controlled and sometimes things may come across harsh, but this shouldn't reflect who you are.

There will be a lot of times that you will want to take things personally, and granted sometimes things are personal because they mean a lot to you. After all, this is your hard work, dedication, and livelihood. But one thing I have learned from someone who meant a lot to me and that I still live by today is "No matter what happens to you, good or bad, it is always what's best for you!" And I know that can be hard at times to believe, but if you can always say that to yourself every time something didn't go as planned, and know there is always something better for you, you will find that you will handle things better and save yourself a lot of grief. You will be surprised how often we are hard on ourselves for something that we have no control over and was not meant for us.

I had a client who I worked with for six years who I loved very much and truly enjoyed working with. But one day, he just stopped working with me. Maybe I will never understand why, and often I blamed myself. When these things happen in this industry, it's often quick and with no explanation, so it can really make you doubt yourself.

But right or wrong, it won't change anything. You can't take it personal; you just have to pick up and keep going. There could be a lot of reasons for this sudden change that may have nothing to do with you. Maybe they just handled it wrong. You just have to believe that everything happens for what's best for you, believe in yourself and the type of person you are, and know you have always done things to the best of your ability.

However, always remain loyal and continue to make sacrifices for your career. At the end of the day, there are no hard feelings. Unfortunately, this is common and ultimately, I had to accept it, working for this client was no longer for me or needed to play a role in my life.

Shortly after, I began to start working more with new clients and traveling more, and I realized that not working for him opened up the time for me to commit to these new opportunities.

On the other hand, let's say you have worked with a new client, and you are hoping to continue to work with him, you see that they are in town and you didn't receive a call. There could be other scenarios as to why you didn't receive a call back. Maybe they got a haircut before they came, or maybe they didn't need one while they were in town, or maybe they don't work with the same manager, so they don't have your contact information. Maybe they have a barber or groomer out here already, or maybe they didn't like your work. Regardless, it's not meant for you and that's okay. Just keep working hard and what will be for you, will be.

I work with a few production companies and a few major record labels. They call me for jobs they know I can handle, and they trust me with. Although I feel comfortable doing anyone and I know I have the skillset for it, they don't always call me for every job they have, and that's okay. I'm sure they have their reasons. It doesn't always have to work out to my advantage. I appreciate all the opportunities they give me, and I show up on time and do my best work possible.

Since we don't always know the reasons why we weren't called back for a job or given an opportunity, there's no reason to feel discouraged.

Taking things personally can break your confidence. It's easier to just take these situations as learning lessons, enjoy the process, become great, and count your blessings!

Work Ethics

Your work ethics are pretty intense with this type of job, so it is essential for you to be reliable, dedicated, and disciplined. It is very unpredictable and requires last-minute schedule changes and unexpected travel. It is sometimes very hard to manage and can feel impossible at times, especially if you have more than one big artist. They are usually all busy and at different times. Luckily, 90 percent of the time I could juggle four big artists at the same time with insane schedules and still work at the shop in between. I have to tell you though, if you do this, you will be working every single day with no days off. Literally.

Sometimes you might think you finally have a day off, and you get a call for an artist or one of your artists will call and you have to go; being dependable can make all the difference in getting or keeping a client. It's not always easy to be available every single time they call, and you will probably be moving things around to make it happen. From time to time when it's out of your control, and you can't make it, it will be understood—if it rarely happens.

So, you have to make sure this does not occur often, because they may really like you and you may do a great job, but if you are not dependable, they will have to use someone else, or they may ask you if have anyone else you trust to send, and let's be honest, do you want to send someone else? That could very well be the end of your job. I learned that the hard way.

I had a client who I started with when he was a new artist. I was with him for about two years. I did house calls for him, and we did a couple of music videos. Every time he needed me, I was there, but as he became busier and busier with new projects coming out, I was working with a lot of other artists and my schedule was packed. He called me for a haircut at least eight times, and I couldn't go. Granted these calls were at the last minute, and I couldn't arrange my schedule to make it, but it still needed to be done. I explained to him that I really wanted to be there and that he couldn't call me at the last minute because my schedule is too crazy to adjust at the last minute and I also needed time to be able to make it there.

During this time, I ran into him late one night in the studio at two in the morning when I was there setting up to cut another client, and he walked in and said, "What the f#!k!"

I said, "I told you my schedule is crazy. I know I'm fired."

He said, "You're not fired; you're the best, T."

Relieved, I said, "Look, the next time you call me I'm going to drop what I'm doing and come."

He called me about a week later and I couldn't go; I was snowed in, in Pittsburgh, PA, with one of my other clients. I was so upset, but what could I do? He never called me again; understandable. Now he is a huge artist, and I am such a fan and wish I still worked with him. I see him around every now and then, and there are no hard feelings, but he now has his team established. I still hope to get another opportunity to work with him again. We will see.

But this is how important it is to be available no matter what, and yes, in this situation I couldn't have possibly made it, but I shouldn't have let it get this far. I should have made the sacrifice sooner because there are only so many times you can be unavailable.

Things in this business need to keep moving, and they will move with or without you. Do not take your opportunities for granted! Try to plan your schedule out to the best of your ability, and if you have something coming up, make sure you make management aware that you are already committed to certain dates. If possible, offer solutions and try to work it out.

Your schedule will get crazy, and things may need to be moved around, especially if you are still working in a shop. Make sure your shop clients know your schedule could change, and most of the time, they will work with you; just know, you may have to make sacrifices from time to time for them, too.

I remember when I had a day scheduled at the shop and a day off planned as well, and I was in Atlanta heading home. I had another client who needed a last-minute haircut. He had a flight from California to New York, and by the time I would have made it back to California, he would have had to leave, so they bought me a new flight and I had to meet him in New York. Instead of going home like I thought, I was now going to New York for a few days. There went my much needed day off, and I had to rearrange my schedule at the shop. This is a typical day in my life, but as crazy as my life gets, it always works out, and I feel beyond blessed to be able to be in such demand.

If you want to aspire to be in the same industry, I encourage you to follow your dreams. You will have a lot of work ahead of you so just make sure you stay consistent, focused, grounded, and dedicated in order to maintain a solid work ethic.

Making it All Work

Making your schedule work for you can be tough in this business. You have to maintain control of a lot of aspects of your business and personal life to make it all come together smoothly. We will discuss maintaining your schedule with your shop and private clients and dealing successfully with the pressures of the industry.

Maintaining Shop and Celebrity Clients

We just discussed how accessible and dedicated you have to be to your exclusive clients and how it can be chaotic at times maintaining every aspect of your life. I feel that even though you don't get much downtime, it is still important to hold on to all your clients regardless, if they are at the shop or part of your private clientele. I have always continued to work at the barbershop while traveling and working with my artists. I have regular clients who depend on me to cut their hair as well. Some I've had since before I began working in the entertainment industry. They saw me go after my goals, achieve what I wanted to do with my life, and have supported me along the way. I appreciate them, and I love working at the barbershop I am at.

People always ask, –Why do you even work at the shop if you have all these celebrity clients? – Well, I do it for a lot of reasons. First of all, I love the culture of the barbershop, and I still get a lot of my inspiration from there. It keeps me grounded and it allows me to keep up with what goes on in the barber world. It keeps me fluid in my haircuts and up to date with current hair trends and tools. I also love the people I work with and the family we have created there.

As hard as it gets at times to fit everything into my schedule, I wouldn't trade it for the world. I get my normalcy from the shop. I love it, and it is very special to me. I keep it as separate as possible from my Hollywood life, and I like it better this way. I have realized through the glam of it all, I am an introvert and I love a quiet life as well. Plus, I have a pretty good base of clients there that over the years have become like family to me, and it's also very consistent, so I make it work in between my Hollywood clients and traveling.

If you decide to follow this path, try to stay humble and keep your chair at the shop because you can always rely on the shop, and there will always be people that need to have haircuts on a more frequent basis. Yes, you are charging your celebrity clients more, but your shop clients are consistent. If you can swing doing both, do it!

In this industry, you are not guaranteed to be with an artist forever. I've seen that change from one day to the next, and their schedule goes through a lot of different phases as well. For instance, they may be recording an album for a year and just need haircuts from time to time. But then that album releases and they begin promo, so they will be busy and need haircuts more often. Or they could go on tour and either fly you out when they need a haircut, which is usually on an approved schedule or maybe not at all if they can find someone on the road. This can fluctuate so it really just depends on the artist and their needs. An artist may or may not need you for periods at a time, and if he is your only artist, you will need to have another steady income and be in a shop. Every client is different and piecing together a workload that fits your needs can be challenging but worth it because working in a shop is always a reliable source of clients and income.

Another important reason to try your best to maintain a solid client base in a shop is not only for reliability but also for financial security in case you have significant downtime. Having a plan B when it comes to your financial security is a must. Don't get me wrong; it is possible to work with one private client who stays busy enough for you to be exclusive to only him, but they have to be an A-list star who is protective of their privacy and takes care of their team. I know a barber who is an exclusive barber to a major celebrity and is completely happy with it. His client is a huge A-list celebrity, and he makes great money. This particular artist has a personal entourage of people that have been with him for 20 years, including his barber. He is a very private person, so not too many people come in and out, but he takes care of his team, and this barber feels secure enough to know that just being with this one artist works well for him.

On the other hand, I know a barber who had two major artists he was working with and gave up working at the shop to go on tour and cater to them. In the beginning, it was very fun for him, and he was living a great life, until 15 years and two kids of his own down the line, and one of his artists wasn't as big anymore and stopped making music and touring, and the other artist just decided one day he wanted to switch barbers, and just like that, my friend never received another call. No explanation or anything, just no more contact with that client.

Usually, when an artist does this, you no longer cut the team either. Whoever the new barber is will take over everyone. This was very sad for me to see. He ended up going back into the shop but with no clientele and no investments, nor did he create a company or some type of external income to carry him beyond this business. He did not think of this scenario because he felt as though the artist needed him, so he was completely caught off guard. Essentially, he had to start from scratch. This is very difficult coming from living a certain lifestyle to back in the shop, promoting for new clients and answering everyone's questions.

This is why you should always maintain a steady stream of clientele, it's important for you to think ahead for yourself, and your own quality of life.

No matter which of these situations apply to you, you always want to save money and have a plan B. His story kept me grounded and taught me that you have to work smarter and harder to keep your own business going. Don't take anything for granted, think about YOUR future, and make smart decisions along the way. It's important to have faith, know your self-worth, and work hard, but you also want to start creating and think of what's next for you. Look at the bigger picture and build your future accordingly, even while you are working hard right now.

Handling the Pressure

Despite the priceless moments and having a dream job, all of this can be very stressful, and you will take a lot of falls along the way. Because of the fast-paced lifestyle, mentally you could go back and forth with a lot of different issues and be handling multiple things at once. You may not have anyone who really understands what you are going through or be able to offer full support, and that can feel isolating.

I work very hard and only really have time for my family. Although they know how crazy my schedule is, I don't think they fully understand how intense my life really is sometimes. You have to be strong-minded and ready for anything. The only thing that relieves me from my stress is to spend my off time with the people I love or doing something I love to do. Learning to appreciate the small things are important and realizing how valuable your time and energy are, is priceless.

I will be at the shop during the day saying I'm glad I'm off tomorrow, and the next thing I know, I'm on a last-minute flight somewhere that night. Unexpected craziness is the story of my life. I'm sharing so that if this is a dream of yours, you can know exactly what you can expect and how to prepare. If things seem to become overwhelming, remember that the hardest parts of life are when you grow the most!

To stay prepared for any unexpected work nights, always carry your tools with you in case you have to leave at any given moment for work. I recommend having two sets of all of your equipment, so you can leave one at the shop and carry one with you. You always have to stay ready, so I make it a habit to always have my backpack with my clippers everywhere I go.

Also, anytime you are traveling to another state and back in one day, take an overnight bag just in case you have to stay or travel to another location. Also have a prepacked bag ready and in your car for any last minute trips. This can seem extreme, but it is best to be prepared. You will find it will make your life easier and you will be able to be more reliable and efficient.

> *Focus leads to achievement and achievement leads to success.*

Chapter Ten

The Business Side

Once you cultivate the important rules, develop a strong work ethic with professionalism, and learn to manage your business and personal stresses, you will be ready to put your focus on building your business. If you're like me and your goal is to be a Topbarber in the entertainment business then your goal will be to maintain a solid reputation, avoid making mistakes as much as possible, and put your energy into working towards a successful career.

To help prepare you for the financial side of the business, we will discuss understanding your value, setting your rates, what to expect from being on set, house calls and travel, how to invoice for these jobs, as well as incorporating some of the ins-and-outs of the industry and other opportunities that you will have available.

This side of the business will involve some ups and downs and trial and errors. This is expected, so don't be too hard on yourself. It will take time to get familiar with how things operate in this business, but it is critical to succeeding. Distractions will be all around you, so keep your business together and organized, keep your mind in a business mindset, and stay focused. Focus leads to achievement and achievement leads to success.

Understanding Your Value

The first thing you should know as a barber in the entertainment business is your value is immeasurable, and you are very essential. Whatever photoshoot, music video, or event your client has will not happen until they meet with you to be cut, styled, or groomed first. Even if it's just a house call to get freshened up, you make the difference in whether he feels good enough to step out or be photographed.

Unfortunately, at times this industry has a way of making you feel last to be recognized for all of your sacrifices. You may often feel your talent and ability are taken for granted, and you may have to stand up for yourself to get all the credit you deserve, therefore, I'm here to let you know, you are amazing at what you do, and you have just as much credibility as the next person on the artists team. It takes an entire team, including the artist, to make this job successful.

So, because you are necessary and will be making a lot of sacrifices to make sure your job is done efficiently and to the best of your ability, you are entitled to charge what you feel your time and talent is worth. Never forget your talent and effort is valuable and so is your time.

Financial Management

Working as a freelance barber in the entertainment industry comes with its own financial management. While there are some similarities to managing your finances working in a barbershop, you have more to consider in the entertainment industry. Here we will discuss setting your rates for house calls, traveling and while you are on set. Also invoicing for these and keeping track of your work.

Housecall Rates

You will also be charging differently for house calls, traveling, and set rates. When considering your rates, you will need to factor in location, travel, and time. If you're doing a house call and the client is new and you are unsure what to quote, you can always ask them what their normal barber charges and go from there.

I can't tell you what to charge, but for house calls, you can consider what you charge in the shop and add your time and travel. You should make it worth your while, but at the same time, keep it within reason. You don't want to overcharge or undervalue your work and get stuck at a low rate. So, you have to charge for what you and your time are worth, but be careful of overcharging. I have seen some barbers significantly increase the rate because the client is a celebrity, and it is assumed they can afford it. This is true, but I believe it is more about the principle. Barbers that have overcharged lose out on a lot of opportunities, especially if they are new to the game and don't have a reputable status.

If your talent list is extensive and your experience is top tier then charging more for your credibility can be accepted and is expected, but this takes time to build this up. I feel like you should believe in yourself and charge what you think your talent is worth, but you should also be aware of the risk of overcharging. Sometimes it's not about charging a large fee a few times; it's about longevity and opportunity. If you have a valid reason for your rates, discuss them so you can be on the same page.

You are your own boss, so you have to be a boss and take responsibility for these conversations. Your client should know that him, his time, and his image are not only important to you, but are also a priority, and you take your craft and business seriously. If they feel this and love the way you cut their hair, it should not be an issue of what you charge.

Travel Rates

When traveling for a client, your rates can vary, but a lot of times these rates can be discussed with the management and an agreement can be made before you travel, depending on how far you have to go and the amount of work that is being done. For example, I have a client that I fly all over for just to do his beard. I feel bad charging him high rates, but there is a risk in traveling and I'm taking most, if not all, of my day to get to him and back. Yes, it's a beard, and yes, he pays for my flight, driver, and accommodations. Despite the fact it's just a beard, I still have to charge him for all the time and energy it takes for me to get to him; plus, I take into consideration an entire day of no other work getting done.

My time is very valuable and the sacrafices are always great, so this can be overwhelming at times, especially when it's last minute. I don't charge him as much as I would a client with the same travel, that I have to perform a full retwist and line-up on, but I charge him a dayrate to compensate for the time and travel involved, as well as a rate for the service. So, things like this need to be discussed and understood on both sides, but ultimately your time, effort, and talent should be compensated. Later, in this chapter we discuss more about housecalls, rates, reimbursements, and the work it involves when you travel.

Regardless, keep your rates consistent for each client, although you may be charging differently for each one. Whatever you decided to charge each client, write it down and keep these rates consistent for this client for housecalls, studiocalls and regular service travels (this is not for shoots with travel – those rates will be higher– but this way you will know exactly how to charge and what you're charging for).

Honestly, when I first started, I charged each client differently depending on who they were because I had no idea what amount was appropriate, and I'm sure at times I undercharged. Now, throughout the years of learning and building my value, I still have different rates depending on the client and what gigs we have, but I have adjusted my rates to an amount that I feel my value is compensated and I feel appreciated for my talent.

Set Rates

With set rates, while working with celebrity clients and dealing with record labels or production on big professional sets, just remember to stand up for yourself, your rates, and your talent. If you don't have someone to negotiate for you, don't be afraid to discuss rates if you feel you should be paid more. Before I started Topbarber Agency I was handling all of my own negotiations myself, and it was hard for me to determine if I was overcharging or under cutting myself.

In this industry you have to say what you want, or you won't get it. As long as you have a valid reason for your rates you will probably get what you ask for. Sometimes production will try to offer you a low amount just to see if you will take it. I find this insulting and I try to stick to my rates, especially if I'm offering full grooming and it is an overnight video or a full day. Granted, you may have a lot of downtime throughout the day but your hours on set add up regardless of the amount of time spent waiting.

If this is your first time working for a particular artist and someone asks you if you are available to do a shoot and you are unsure what to charge, you can ask what the budget is. When they tell you, if you like the rate accept it quickly. If you don't, you should consider who the client is, how long the shoot will be and the amount of work you have to do in order to quote a rate for the day. I would write down customary rates for my services considering all these factors and work around these.

Sometimes this takes experience and time, but if you keep track of your jobs and rates, it will be no time before you feel comfortable having these conversations and asking for a reasonable but acceptable rate without jeopardizing losing a job to someone who is willing to take a lower rate.

This is where your credibility and work ethic come into play, they know they will get what they pay for, so if you are constantly building your professionalism, creative talent, portfolio, likability, being a team player, roster of clients and always maintaining set etiquette, you will be worth them making the decision to choose you.

One thing to remember is in this business word of mouth is what will get you your next job, because they go by trust of the people that are involved in production or management so everything you do in this business is built around your work ethic, reputation, and your ability to negotiate.

If you work privately for a client and he requests you to be on set with him, you can ask his management who is paying for you to be there. If the artist is paying, I would charge him a standard rate that is worth my time and service, but I wouldn't take advantage. However, if it is not the artist paying, when they ask you for your rates, its always better to come in high so that you can negotiate down, if need be. Typically, if production is paying you, they will pay what they have to because you are his personal barber or groomer. They are aware these artists cannot or possibly will not perform or shoot if they do not look the part and feel their best. In this situation you do have leverage because the artist is requesting you. If your artist is paying you, be reasonable because you want your artists management to know you are a team player and that they can always feel they can have you there with him without having to pay an outrageous rate. This also opens up future opportunities for the label to call you for other artists they manage as well.

Since your rate can vary when dealing with production or other on camera jobs your client may be asked to do, another option to make it easy is to find a dayrate (a standard rate you will charge for a half day or full day), with consideration to the hours involved, the services you will provide and travel time to and from the location. These rates will most likely be higher.

At the end of the day, it has to be a win win for everyone involved and if you can manage this you will be a success in no time and you will have an impressive portfolio and career to be proud of.

So, remember to keep track of what you charge for each client. Although rates can vary, do your best to keep them consistent for housecalls, travel, photoshoots, videos, and anything else they may have.

Remember you are charging professional rates so be professional, dependable, on time, prepared, confident, and most of all irreplaceable.

Creating Invoices

After doing a house call, sometimes the artist will pay you directly, but when you are on set or traveling, you will have to submit an invoice before you can get paid. Sometimes this can take anywhere from a few days to a few weeks, so be prepared to wait. Keep track and pay attention to all your invoices and what money you have floating around, and mark them paid soon as they come in. Usually, when you have been with an artist for a while, you will be put on payroll (this is when you are paid through direct deposit) from his finance people, usually within a few days. If you are on payroll, you will be submitting an invoice every time you show up for him.

However, if production or the label is paying your invoice, this will take longer, because along with an invoice for the first time, you most likely will have to submit a W-9 and/or your bank account information. This usually takes a couple of weeks but sometimes sooner. Invoices are kind of difficult at first, but you just have to find a good invoice app that you can use directly from your phone or invest in something like QuickBooks to help you keep track of everything throughout the year, because once you become really busy, you want this to be as simple as possible. I complete my invoices on the job, so I don't forget, and if I need any information, the people I need to ask are right there.

Once you get used to doing and submitting your invoices, over time it gets easy. Learning and being consistent with your invoices shows others your business and professionalism matter to you, it's all a part of being your own boss.

On The Go

Being on the go can add a whole new busyness to your life. You will have to be prepared for long busy days on set, last-minute house calls and unexpected travel. It sounds exciting, but it is a lot of work. There is a lot that goes into staying prepared and there's a lot of responsibility to endure on these jobs. The pressure can sometimes be intimidating, but with a little preparedness, you can be ready for anything!

Let's discuss what life on set, doing house calls, and traveling entails and how to make it go as smoothly as possible.

Life On Set

From the very beginning, it has been an interesting challenge figuring out everything as I went. For instance, when we were doing music videos, production would hire someone for hair and makeup for everybody including the artist. But I would show up for my artist and often people would look confused and would ask my client, "You brought your own barber?" We got this a lot as we showed up to set, as if this was not normal. Also, on the call sheets, they had to be made aware that he was bringing his own barber, and when we received the call sheet before each video, it would say "Hair" or "Barber" next to my name.

After some time, I started to include making sure his face was looking fresh as well, I incorporated things he needed like lotions, lip balm, light powder, etc. This made me more valuable, more in demand, and increased my income significantly. It set me apart from everyone else. I realized I needed a title that better conveyed my role, so I decided I would refer to myself as the groomer and be specific about what I offered. It took a while to stick but now that is the title when you are hair and light makeup for a male.

Not all artists like makeup but you are required to make them look fresh and clean for each shot and have anything else hygiene related from face wipes, moisturizer, deodorant, fingernail clippers, eye drops etc. Anything you can think of they may ask for is good to have on hand. This was an interesting process for me. There aren't too many barbers that are groomers, so you will definitely add value to yourself if you can offer this service.

Before your day begins on any set you will receive a callsheet before each production, this is paperwork you will have emailed to you prior to the production day. This will have all pertinent information pertaining to the day including your call time, which is the time you should arrive, your clients call time, location, scheduled shots for the day and anything else you should know. You may have to email back confirming you have received the callsheet, make sure you do, and also make sure you read it! It is very important.

When you are at events such as videos, commercials, editorials, award shows, red carpet, etc. You have to come prepared. Be sure to always arrive on set an hour before your client so you have time for any delays, like finding parking or having to shuttle to the location. You should always be set up and ready by the time your client arrives. It is unprofessional if you show up at the same time or late.

Any time they will be on camera for an extended amount of time, you will have to be ready to groom them at a moment's notice. Make sure you are paying attention and be ready to do any last looks, which is last minute touches on client before camera rolls. This also includes making sure they look camera-ready in between wardrobe changes before each new scene. Make sure you have everything your client likes such as lip balm, lotion, hair products, etc. and have it easily accessible in your set bag.

You should keep list of the things that each client prefers so you have anything they might want set up for them when they arrive. This shows that you are professional, and you care about their needs and what they like. Make sure you have a set bag to carry with you to keep all your necessities in. This is a bag that you will have everything you use for that client that you will pre-pack and carry with you at all times while you are on set. Be sure to consider the weather if you are shooting outside and customize your bag according to that. Your bag will typically include brush or comb, lip balm, small lotion, powder, powder brush, hand sanitizer, oil blotting sheets, paper towels, hand wipes, bottled water, and anything else you use often for that client.

They are all different and they all like certain brands. Make your bag is customized to that client. If this is a new client for you, reference him and carry your basics plus anything you may need according to the reference.

If a new job is being offered to you, then be competitive with your rates because they may go with someone else. If you are doing full grooming, you can charge double what you would to just cut them but take into consideration how many hours the set will run, or you could always charge a day rate you are comfortable with. If someone questions your price, be ready to tell them all that is included and focus on the value you provide to the client.

You will sometimes have to turn down work or take a lower rate if you feel the job is worth it for you in the long run. There will be a lot of things to take into consideration, but it has to make sense.

As your reputation grows, you will not be questioned about your rates if you build a professional reputable status. This will take years of hard consistent work and building solid relationships, but it is all worth it and you will stay busy.

Part of being successful in this industry not only requires being professional but it also means you need to be on top of your creative skills, performing your best possible work, a team player and being able to bring visions to reality. There will be treatments available for you to look at, this is basically a pictured story giving you the details of the shoot, including looks and visuals.

However, you never know what will be required on set or which creative direction an artist will go, so be ready to adapt to changing trends and visions that may be hard to achieve. This is when your creativity and skill come into play. I suggest you educate yourself and take classes or workshops whenever possible to help keep you fluid in your skills and enhance your arsenal of talents.

Housecalls and Travel

Housecalls are a service that you will provide to your exclusive clientele who are most likely too popular or too busy to go to a shop. They will pay more for you to come to them. Housecalls are not easy because you are traveling to a location, finding somewhere to set up your equipment, complete the service, cleaning up after, packing up, and going to your next location. You are not in your typical setting with good lighting and a mirror. You are also setting your equipment up on a chair, table, dresser, couch, pretty much anywhere you can. You are always making adjustments, so because of these unorthodox settings, you will most likely take longer to complete your haircuts. Aside from all of your tools and products, always remember to bring a headlamp so you can see pretty well under any circumstances and an extension cord in case you are far from an outlet.

Traveling can be time-consuming as well, depending on where you're going and if you are staying overnight. When you travel, I would charge a dayrate according to your overall time commitment. I live in California and if I need to fly to Las Vegas, I can go cut my client and come right back and it will take a half-day. But if I have to fly to Atlanta or New York and come right back, it will take the entire day. Charge accordingly.

Usually, all of your expenses are covered, and you can be reimbursed if you have to pay for anything like an Uber or airport parking. Most of the time you will have a driver at the airport waiting to pick you up to take you to your hotel or directly to the artist, the discretion is up to your client. Usually, you will work all the details out with management.

When you fly make sure you pack as light as possible and try not to check a bag, as bags can get lost and sometimes you won't have time to go to baggage claim.

Also, packing your clippers are fine but do not take any shears over five inches, and do not carry a full pack of new blades, if TSA finds them, they will make you throw them away, check your bag or confiscate them. This will create an unnecessary delay or a problem. I usually put a blade or two somewhere in my luggage but totally separate from my razor.

Also, make sure you don't have a blade inside your razor. If you don't follow TSA regulations and they find your razor with a blade in it, they will throw your entire razor away! If need be, you can ask management if they can have blades for you when you arrive or allow time for you to go get them.

Also, follow TSA rules for approved liquids, and don't forget to bring your headlamp and extension cord. Take a picture of the terminal you parked in, leave a parking ticket inside your car, keep all your receipts, and have a safe and productive trip!!

Regardless, if you are doing house calls or traveling on the road once you arrive your attention and priority is on your client. Your time revolves around your client, and it is important that you make sure he is taken care of first before you tend to anything else.

Industry Option

Instead of controlling every aspect of your career, there are other directions you can go that can be a great change. As we talked about earlier being your own boss, attaining an agent like Topbarber Agency who can pick up a lot of the responsibility for you or getting into the Union for TV and Film may spark a new creative direction for you. Let's discuss it a little more.

Work for Yourself or Get an Agent

You can take a lot of routes in this industry. You can be like me and work independently with high-profile clients, where you do your own networking, negotiations, and handle your own schedule, invoices, and charge your own prices. Or you could get an agent who works for an agency such as Topbarber Agency who basically has the access to get you gigs, doing major commercials, A-list photoshoots, editorials, etc.

Major companies often like to reach out to agencies they are familiar with to send them hair and makeup people because they are not so worried about paying more than they are for looking for someone who understands the rules, is professional and has the credentials to do the job they are expecting. Along with sealing the deal for you, agents also handle your rates, make sure you are treated well on set, handle any problems, and submit invoices for payment. They try and get you the highest paid jobs because they do get a percentage, and these jobs are usually reputable and are hard to get on your own.

In some reputable agencies their agents will have full control of your schedule, although they discuss it with you, they are in control of all your jobs. So, any clients you work with are booked through them and they get a percentage of it all. They will negotiate all your rates, getting you paid top dollar, whether you have been working with a client previously or not, and they are also more likely to start charging your personal clients more as well, so you would have to be willing to take that risk. If you plan on working in a shop, depending how busy your agent keeps you, make sure you stay ahead of your schedule as much as possible so you can book your clients accordingly.

For me, it's quite the change; having an agent doesn't work because I have too many clients, and the change will interrupt my schedule too much. Because of this reason, I made my agency not take over your complete schedule of clients, but we do expect if you commit to a job you show up, follow Topbarber expectations and represent the company with professionalism and to the best of your ability. If this is something you want to look into, keep working on your versatility, start taking pictures and put together a professional online portfolio. Keep track of the opportunities you are getting outside the shop because you have to show experience to be picked up by an agency. If this is what you are interested in, go for it!

The Union for Tv and Film

There is another side to this industry, and that is the Union (in my area, it's the 706 Union supported by IATSE). This is for the tv and film industry from sitcoms to movies. The Union will represent you and post jobs when they are available. These jobs usually go on for a duration of time, depending on how long the project is.

You are scheduled to be there for a certain amount of time each day and can even require relocating, this depends on the job being offered. You are not required to take all jobs, so this makes it flexible to your schedule and what you are willing to take. The union protects you from different issues and provides paid overtime, holiday pay, essential rest, and they pretty much make sure you are treated right according to their standards. The union also offers great medical and pension benefits, that's why most hairstylists join. However, there are only a few ways to join:

One way is the 60–60–60. You complete 60 days of non-roster work experience in each three years of work, within the last five-year period. In Los Angeles County this will be on sets such as network television, music videos, or non-union films or television productions.

If you want to go this route, it is important to know that when you join the union, you will qualify under either hair or makeup. At the moment they don't have barbering, so if you are a barber, you will qualify under makeup to do men's grooming. If you have your cosmetologist license, you qualify under hair and you can do women's and men's grooming. If you have dual licenses (both barber and cosmotologist); this would be a great opportunity for you to have some flexibility.

If you're only doing or just starting to do music videos and eventually want to apply for the union, make sure your name is on all the call sheets under hair or grooming so you can get the credit for it. This will all be counted towards your days.

You can also apply for the union if you have worked on one set for 30 consecutive days. Not 28 or 29, it has to be 30 or more or it won't count. Or, if the main actor or artist who is scheduled to be in the movie requests you to be on set with him, you can then be allowed to work on a union job and then apply to be in the union if you choose, after. But you have to show proof that you have worked with this actor or artist before on set for some time for this to be approved.

You also have to pay your initiation dues to join. This is a one-time payment. It's a bit pricy, at this current time it is $6,000 for makeup, and $5,500 for hair. They require half down and the other half to be paid in six months. After initiation, the dues to remain working are $262.97 and must be paid quarterly on or before January 1st, April 1st, July 1st, and October 1st. Any member who accepts work and is behind in their payments is subject to fines.

This is a responsibility, but the money you make and the benefits you get make it worth it. You are not required to take every job that comes up, but they make sure you get offered enough so you can afford to pay your dues. A lot of people like the movie and television industry because of the stability and the benefits, which as you know as independent contractors we don't get on our own. However, like with any job, these projects can have long hours with the same people until that job is over.

These are all exciting avenues you can aspire to take on, just remember to move with purpose and prepare yourself throughout your journey. I wish you much success in all of your career choices, creative accomplishments and becoming a Topbarber.

Chapter Eleven

From The Heart

At this point in my life, I have been on the go for the last 10 years in an insanely busy, demanding industry and I have to say I have accomplished more in these last 10 years than I ever have in my entire life. It's been a wild journey and I have learned many valuable lessons along the way. I am forever grateful for my talent, but more for my perseverance, strength, guidance, and the protection I have received along the way.

I have realized that my ultimate goal is to contribute to something beyond myself and to inspire barbers to do whatever it is they want to do within this extraordinary industry, and to encourage them to keep working hard and follow their dreams even when the journey gets difficult.

I hope that through reading this book, you have learned that no matter what happens, where you go, or how many shops you decide to work in, nobody can take away anything you have acquired along the way. Anywhere you go, your expertise and experience will always go with you.

This is where taking the time to invest in yourself becomes so priceless. I know the many paths you can take in the barber industry can be a lot to take in and consider; but it is such a rewarding challenge. I sincerely hope every chapter in this book has helped to give you some insight, knowledge and encouragement to become a better you.

I hope you realize all of your setbacks are inside of you, and it's up to you to push through for a higher success. Even if your dream seems like it's just a dream, believe in yourself, be persistent, stay focused and keep going. You will receive everything you are asking for; it is how the universe works. Be patient and don't worry about how, just be ready for when. There is always a new chapter in life; don't be afraid to start it!

This book is my new chapter, and I hope it helps you find inspiration, motivation, and passion within your purpose so you can also inspire others. As barbers we have something special to offer, and we can make this world a better place. We all have a purpose in life; it's up to us to find it, live it, and share it — Be a Topbarber.

Tracy Love

Be A Topbarber.

COME SEE US!!
Tik Tok: @beatopbarber
Instagram: @topbarberagency
Website: Topbarberagency.com

PLEASE USE THE FOLLOWING PAGES TO WRITE DOWN ANY GOALS OR IDEAS YOU MAY HAVE AND TAKE NOTES!

Goals

Goals

Ideas

Ideas

Ideas

Notes

Notes

Notes

Acknowledgments

First and foremost, I would like to thank you God for always protecting me and my family and being there when I needed to talk. Thank you for giving me everything I asked for when you knew I was ready to receive it. I would not be who I am without you. I am grateful and forever thankful.

I would like to thank my family for being the backbone of my success:

Sherah~ Thank you for being the big sister and holding the house together through all my late nights and traveling, my journey would not have been possible without you, and I appreciate you and love you so much for all the sacrifices you have made for me, thank you for being the special, supportive, encouraging, and loving person you are.

Kaaria~ thank you for being the sweet, beautiful, smart and talented young lady you have grown into, and for your support all these years. Thank you for being the photographer in the family and taking the picture for the cover of this book, it means the world to me.

Tory~ Thank you for your support as well son, and for not driving everyone crazy. You have grown into an amazing man and I couldn't be more proud of you. You are a super special talented young man with a lot of drive and passion for what you do. Thank you for the music for the trailer for this book it means so much. I am super proud and excited for you and I can't wait to hear how you change the world.

Jaedyn, Ryan and Riley you guys are something else, but I love you with all my heart!! You all have been there every single day supporting me throughout my journey and I love you so much and I am so thankful for you guys! I love you all forever.

Mom~ Thank you for all the conversations on my long drive home and being there for me when I felt no one would understand. I want to thank you for all your sacrafices you have made for me and everything you have done for me throughout my life. I get my hard work, independent, conscientious mindset from you, and I am thankful for you making me into who I am. I love you!

Nipsey Hussle~ Thank you forever for helping me continue my purpose and inspiring me to write this book, you have changed my life.

To my Chops family~ Cynthia you are the best boss, thank you for being who you are, we need more people like you in this world. I appreciate you for letting me use the barbershop picture for the back of this book, it really means a lot! And to all the barbers, thank you guys for being such good friends and supporting me throughout my writing process and my crazy life. We have been through a lot together and we always stick together that's why I love being there. I honestly don't think there's another shop like us. I love you guys.

To my clients~ I am grateful for you all, thank you for all the great conversations, laughs, and allowing me into your lives. Some of you have been there from the beginning and I appreciate you for all your patience and dedication throughout the years.

Thank you for believing in me and trusting me with your hair.

Biography

Tracy Love is a licensed barber and cosmetologist that specializes in men's haircare. She has been in this amazing industry over 20 years. She has moved throughout her career with the intention to master haircutting and perfect her craft. In 2021 she started the first barber/male grooming agency called Topbarber, where barbers are sent to do housecalls, videos, photoshoots, editorials, commercials and more. She takes pride in giving opportunities to barbers who want to elevate their career to the next level.

She has done Hair Shows up and down the Westcoast, including Las Vegas and Arizona doing platform work and private educational classes for one the biggest clipper companies in the world, Andis, for 6 years.

She has also made her mark in the Entertainment Industry for more than 10 years and counting, working with some of the biggest Music Artists in the world including Wiz Khalifa, Big Sean, Juicy J, 2Chainz, Travis Scott, Russ, Soulja Boy, Chris Brown, Ty Dolla$ign, Swae Lee, Mike Posner, and more! She has also worked with TV greats such as O'Shea Jackson Jr., Ice Cube, Ice T, Billy Dee Williams and more. Together she has done Talk Shows such as Ellen, Jimmy Kimmel, The Tonight Show, Good Morning America, Ridiculousness, Revolt TV, The Real, The New Arsenal Hall Show, and Red Carpet for A-listed Filmed Events for TV.

She has done tons of Music Videos and Editorials for just about every Entertainment and Fashion Magazine including the Double Cover Power 30 Issue of Source Magazine, GQ, Vogue Italy and Playboy.

She has also done Commercials for Adidas, Gatorade and more, including two Super Bowl Commercials for Pepsi and T-Mobile, along with Award Shows Including the Grammy's, BET Awards, MTV Video Music Awards, BillBoard Music Awards, and iHeart Radio Music Awards including The Grammy's tribute to 50 Years in HipHop.

She has traveled across the United States doing what she has so much passion for and working for people she is inspired by. Above all her successes this book is by far the most challenging yet rewarding achievement.

And although her life is priceless and her time is of most value, there is no where she would rather be than at home with her family, who are the heartbeat for all of her hard work.

Check out my Portfolio on topbarberagency.com!

And join me on Tik Tok @beatopbarber for barber discussions and new releases!!

Thank you for purchasing this book, hopefully I will see you at upcoming shows or events, to answer any questions you may have about this book!!

Please check the Topbarber website for updates!!

Made in the USA
Middletown, DE
14 March 2024